The GABILANS *to* CHOSUN

Memoir of a Forgotten War

S TEPHEN A. KLOTZ

Copyright © 2022 Stephen A. Klotz

All rights reserved. No part of this book may be reproduced, stored, or transmitted by any means—whether auditory, graphic, mechanical, or electronic—without written permission of both publisher and author, except in the case of brief excerpts used in critical articles and reviews. Unauthorized reproduction of any part of this work is illegal and is punishable by law.

ISBN: 978-1-957203-35-5 (sc)
ISBN: 978-1-957203-36-2 (hc)
ISBN: 978-1-957203-37-9 (e)

Because of the dynamic nature of the Internet, any web addresses or links contained in this book may have changed since publication and may no longer be valid. The views expressed in this work are solely those of the author and do not necessarily reflect the views of the publisher, and the publisher hereby disclaims any responsibility for them.

The Ewings Publishing LLC
One Galleria Blvd., Suite 1900, Metairie, LA 70001
1-888-421-2397

CONTENTS

Foreword v
Introduction ix

Book I
Army Bound

An Army Reception 3
Basic Training 6
A Mexican Interlude 11
Advanced Infantry Training 15
The Female PFC 22
Tell Me All About It 26
Nietzsche 30
Pacinni 33
Weekend in Lawton 36
"Who do you think you are?" 38
Preface to Book II 43

Book II
Life Near the DMZ, First Year (1966)

Santa Barbara 47
Arriving at 1/17th Field Artillery 52
Field Exercise 55
The "Gooks" 58
"We're not going to kill anybody!" 62
"Gentlemen, grab your drinks" 71
"God Damn It, why don't you play right?" 75
Doctor Zhivago 80

A Fiasco 85
Frog and an Eighth Army Exercise 91
Mona 96
Frog Cracks Up 104
Now is the time to speak of Major Puff.................... 106
Disgraced 113
Special Weapons 118
Daily Life Near the DMZ 122
The Motor Pool 129
The Swap 133
Lapse of Judgment... 140
The Mess is Inspected 142
The *Pueblo* and the Blue House............................. 146
Seoul 150
Each Day Became an Eternity 155
Goodbye to Chosun 157
Coming Home 158
Epilogue 159

FOREWORD

Alongside the run up to full-scale war in Vietnam in the late Nineteen Sixties tens of thousands of American boys were also sent to the Republic of Korea. Colloquially termed South Korea, it was a rugged and desolate land. Americans back home knew little about it other than a war had been waged there a generation before. The public as well as the news media were ignorant of the ongoing American military struggles below the 38th Parallel.

A young soldier embarking for Korea in those benighted times, running into a soldier who had been stationed there, would ask, "What's it like?" the response invariably was, "Sure beats Nam!" The following pages are one man's story of service in Chosun, the Land of the Morning Calm.

DEDICATION

To A.P. and M.P.K. who made the All of me.
They should be been given all the credit
for what good I have achieved.

INTRODUCTION

In the fall of 2004 Dr. Paul Caanen flew to Monterey, California to attend an AIDS conference. He rented an economy model sedan and placed a roll of watercolor paper, a glass jar, brushes and several tubes of paint in the backseat and then drove out of town to paint landscapes before the meeting the following day. Driving toward Salinas alongside the Santa Lucia Mountains, he carefully pulled off the pavement next to a recently disked field. He placed the watercolor paper on the trunk, sketched the mountain slope before him with its scattered live oaks. A white farmhouse and red barn stood out halfway up the mountainside. His feet slumped into the soft dirt, meadowlarks called from clumps of rust-colored grass at the edge of the field and the late morning sun warmed his tall frame.

An hour later, he tossed out the water, placed the painting on the back seat and drove toward Fort Ord, a site he had not seen for over thirty years. He went through the main gate, now derelict, and looked toward a small cluster of decaying barracks. These buildings once stood shoulder-to-shoulder, block following block, in the immense fort. Nearby, was the dilapidated Fort Theatre with a fabric banner billowing out in the gentle breeze which read, "Native American Rally Today". When Caanen last saw the theater it was advertising "The Sound of Music."

Caanen drove onto an old deserted parade ground, stopped the car, got out and walked along the row of decrepit two-story barracks. Each one rested on pier and beam foundations several feet off the ground. Flakes of yellow-brown paint and fragments of green asbestos shingles lay in neat rows below the buildings, having slid off the gabled roofs. Caanen rapidly sketched the barracks.

Later, he looked westward as the sun just barely topped the pine trees spraying light over the weathered, yellow facades of the barracks. He stepped on to a concrete threshold, pushed open the front door, and entered a small foyer. The stairwell to the second floor was directly in front of him but the wooden floor had a large gaping hole and the flooring had fallen to earth below. Against the gypsum wallboard was a large black plastic bag filled with yellowing paper. Caanen pulled out a stapled contract: a copy of a mortgage for a house in Arkansas. Another sheet with foxed edges was a Department of Defense order cut August 15, 1965, for a staff sergeant to proceed to Kimpo Airport, the Republic of Korea. Caanen stood transfixed trying to recall the moment he had received just such an order. Those were confusing times. He slowly dropped the papers and walked to the car. To the east, just barely perceptible, were the peaks of the Gabilan Range, home to Steinbeck's "Red

Pony." He pulled the automobile keys from his trouser pocket and slid into the front seat staring at the shabby yellow buildings. There was a time when the scene before him was vibrant with thousands of shouting young men, marching and running in formation. Those were exciting times for many men.

BOOK I

Army Bound

AN ARMY RECEPTION

The summer of 1965 was an inferno in the Midwest with daily temperatures nearly 100⁰F throughout June. Paul Caanen, aged 20 dropped out of college for the third time, living at the family farm near Kansas City with his parents. His father, a professor of medicine, was not pleased to see him back in the house and the two argued daily. His father gave up urging his son to return to college and succeed as he had done being awarded a scholarship to the University of Chicago. To show his indifference to his father's achievements, Paul focused his attention on agricultural matters at the farm such as mowing pastures, tending to the sheep, cattle and hogs. His cherished hero was Gabriel Oak from *Far from the Madding Crowd*. Yet, Paul obviously wanted more than just being strong, steady and capable. By night he read the philosophy of Kant and Schopenhauer. It was no surprise however, when he received a letter from the local draft board ordering him to report to the Armed Forces Receiving Center across the street from the Kansas City Post Office, a short stroll from Union Station. Paul's beloved mother drove him to the building in the early morning hours and left him on the sidewalk in his best Levis and T-shirt. She sat in the faux, wood-paneled Mercury station wagon, tears streaming down her cheeks. Caanen, close to tears himself, waved goodbye surreptitiously and walked into the yellow brick building. He felt supremely empty. Yet, he had betrayed his mother by doing absolutely nothing to save himself from this fate. This was not the future she foresaw when leaving him as a freshman at college three years before. As a young bride she had experienced the absence of her husband for three years when he fought his way through Normandy with the 3rd Army; she was not prepared to experience such anxieties again.

A corporal stationed at the entrance told him to find a place to sleep for the night, as he would be boarding a bus the following morning for Ft. Leonard Wood, Missouri and Army Basic Training. After claiming a weathered leather couch to lie on for the night, Paul joined the other recruits assembled in the spacious "ballroom".

"Alright, everyone toes on the yellow line on the floor and face me," shouted a thin, dark haired, stoop-shouldered Specialist E-5. "We're gonna give you a physical and check your blood and urine. Keep your mouths shut and move quickly. Okay, You, You, and You into the latrine and give me a urine sample in this container. Fill it halfway up! Halfway up! I don't want any piss dribbling down the side of the container."

Fifteen minutes later the Specialist slapped a flashlight in his palm to accentuate his commands. "Alright, we're gonna' start the physical. Strip down to your birthday suit and throw your clothes on the chair behind you." There was pandemonium as a hundred men groaned, mumbled profanities and began to remove their clothing. Most of the recruits had never undergone a physical examination and were a little alarmed at what might be coming.

"Hold the noise down! Alright, Doc will check you out for heart murmurs now." Dr. Leon was a short man with large glasses, a menacing smile and graying short-cropped hair. He pronounced his name with a French pronunciation, "Lee-own.' He sauntered casually along the line of men, briefly held the stethoscope to their chest, thrust his head toward the recruit's head and looked him over from head to toe.

"You! Back up two steps and stand there," he said to a recruit after listening intently with the stethoscope. Later he said, "Specialist, collect those men I had fall out and send them back upstairs, they won't be in This Man's Army." A handful of recruits grabbed their clothes, dressed hurriedly, and ran up the stairs to the entrance. No one stopped to argue about the decision—they had been given their freedom because of a heart murmur. Paul was relieved that he had made the cut—it was no use returning home to haphazardly study philosophy and argue with his father, no matter how sophisticated and righteous it made him feel.

"Alright everyone, turn around and face the back of the room. Grab your cheeks and bend over! Bend over there! Doc's gonna check you out for hemorrhoids." The Specialist walked deliberately along the line of men shining the flashlight at each butt. "Dr. Lee-own" walked stiffly behind him glancing over his right shoulder at the straining recruits.

At the close of the day the remaining recruits formed up again on the line in the "ballroom".

"Alright, one man at a time, knock and enter the Doc's office. One at a time! If he gives you the green light, you're off to Leonard Wood tomorrow," the Specialist said.

Paul knocked on the thin paneled door and entered the room with its scuffed, white linoleum tile floor and gun barrel gray government-issue metal desk in the center of the spacious room. Sitting behind the desk, Doctor Leon stared at a document, his right hand buried in the middle desk drawer.

"Are you a muff diver?" he asked, not looking up.

"What, Sir?" Paul asked.

"I said, are you a muff diver!?" Paul, uncertain as to his meaning, looked quizzically at the Doctor who now raised his head. Paul could see he was fingering a pistol in the drawer of the desk. "A muff diver or Nancy-boy, which is it?"

"Muff diver, Sir," Paul said, at which point Dr. Leon signed a form and handed it to him.

BASIC TRAINING

The next morning the recruits boarded the Greyhound buses with their only possessions, the clothes they were wearing. Upon arrival at Ft. Leonard Wood the young men queued for the "barbers." Boot camp began. With raw, shaven and sometimes bleeding skulls, they double-timed over to the quartermaster and were issued fatigues. A Sergeant stood rigidly in front of the men and began chanting, "Alright, I want you to take 4 fatigue trousers, 4 blouses, 8 pairs of socks, one web belt, 8 briefs, 8 tee-shirts... Hey, Asshole I said 8 socks, not 9!" Army efficiency was evident from the get-go. Hundreds of men were measured for summer wardrobes within a matter of minutes and nearly every item fit perfectly.

Their Drill Sergeant met them outside the quartermaster warehouse. He would be with them 24-hours a day for the next two months. Every recruit was immediately in awe of his Drill Sergeant from the moment of the first meeting. Sergeant Powell stood out by virtue of his starched and pressed fatigues, a campaign hat cocked forward on his brow, dark sunglasses that were never removed, and the perfect symmetry of his black facial features and moustache.

Week 1 was an eye opener and Powell's cleverness was inexhaustible. The platoon fell out on the parade ground one very hot afternoon and Powell talked to the men in conversational tones for the first time. He stood at ease, slowly bobbing forward and backward at the waist by rising on his toes. His dark glasses kept everyone from observing where he was looking. He did not sweat like the recruits who had moisture stains under their armpits and down their backsides. His fatigues were always crisply dry, tailored and sharply creased.

"Okay, we need recruits who actually know what they're doing. We've got to get the parade ground renovated this week. Raise your hand if you've driven heavy equipment."

"Good! Fall out over here!"

"How many masons have we got? Fall out over there!" "Any carpenters? Excellent. Fall out over here!"

Most of the platoon volunteered for various 'construction' work. As it turned out "heavy equipment operators" pushed wheelbarrows full of gravel to the parade ground; "masons" were issued a trowel and removed dandelions from the turfed areas; "carpenters" were given crowbars and ordered to remove nails from lumber used to erect the bleachers.

Sgt. Powell's favorite exhortations to the privates under his charge were: "get it right or a Cong's gonna shoot your ass off." "Wake up! You won't last twenty seconds in Nam." "Close up the line, you sons-of-bitches," and "you pansies can double-time it back to the barracks." No one wanted to disappoint his Drill Sergeant and Caanen was no different than the others. Powell's impeccable dress, clear diction and ease around men mesmerized Caanen and the others. To a man, they revered Sgt. Powell.

Caanen was put on KP (Kitchen Police) duty for a week. He spent hours each afternoon peeling spuds, reaching into a burlap sack of potatoes, peeling and cutting out the "eyes" and then pitching the spud into a large galvanized garbage can filled halfway with water. Every now and then the Mess Sgt. inspected the floating potatoes. Caanen and another recruit filled 3 cans a day and struggled to drag the cans into the kitchen. This mass provisioning and the monotony of the job was Caanen's first awareness that life as a private "in this

Man's Army" had its shortcomings. The tedium of daily Army life began to weigh heavily.

The platoon was housed in a brick bungalow-style barrack. The soldiers were busy each evening polishing belt buckles, boots, doorknobs and faucets in the john. Caanen (and every other recruit) spent a lot of energy avoiding Matheny, a bully who sauntered around the barrack in the evenings punching men's shoulders. After an evening of pummeling by Matheny, victims were barely capable of holding their arms in the air. He bullied some soldiers into straightening out his footlocker. Although short statured, Matheny sported enormous biceps.

Calisthenics commenced at 7:00 AM sharp. The exercises were various and Matheny's large biceps could not rescue him from doing poorly in calisthenics. The mile run at the end of the exercise was difficult for him and he gasped for breath. Sgt. Powell was on his case right away. "Come on you pansy, finish the race! For a Tough Guy your legs are puny, Matheny." The other recruits smiled to themselves but hoped the sergeant wouldn't go too far humiliating him—they would be the ones to pay for it.

The heat and humidity were oppressive in cotton fatigues. Afternoon exercises were often called off because of the heat index. Windows were kept open in an effort to prevent the spread of meningitis. Since there was no air conditioning the humidity in the barracks was suffocating. As the second month wore on most of the soldiers lost 10 pounds or more and were constantly hungry. The chow hall was crowded in the evening, but with food, spirits revived. Following dinner everyone drifted back to their barracks and worked on personal matters until Taps. Then, they lay in their briefs on top of the bed sheets—twisting from side to side until dawn.

Private Whaley came from a small family farm in southern Missouri and was the only man in the company with whom Caanen spoke to with regularity. Boot camp was not a place for making friends—recruits were busy from Reveille to Taps—and little was said except for jokes or complaints about the military. Whaley was convinced that everyone would end up in Vietnam. The memory of his small girls waving to him as he left the induction center came to his mind's eye every day.

Caanen, on the other hand, appeared unfazed by threats of being shipped off to Vietnam. The emptiness he felt when his mother left him at the Recruiting Station had been replaced with a gung-ho approach to the Army—he was obsessed with the thought he would make it a career. At night he continued his former way of life reading Nietzsche and Schopenhauer, intellectualizing about his existence. Didn't Wittgenstein volunteer for the Army as a lowly private in World War I and later as a hospital orderly during World War II?

"I don't think I can possibly go to Vietnam," said Whaley. "I mean my wife and girls need me for years to come."

"I doubt the Army is going to consider that a good enough reason for not sending you," Caanen said. Like most of the unmarried men he was not very empathetic. Flushed with his own good health, he was responsible only for himself. He retreated into philosophical sophistry to explain his failure to succeed at the university. He was going to do something different and more important than his father. Whaley's family crisis was not his intimate concern.

Whaley, white-haired and flushed from a day in the sun, looked downcast. He knew full well there would be no exceptions made for him. "My wife wanted me to come home this weekend—they wouldn't give me a pass."

In the Army Caanen and the others experienced a classroom different from any they had known before. Soldiers marched and double-timed from one 'classroom' to the next. Classes were conducted outside in the grueling sun—the lecturers stood on wooden platforms at a rostrum and used microphones. On each side of the platform were flags and guidons of the different units.

The 'students' sat on wooden planks and impatiently awaited their smoke breaks.

One weekend of leave near the end of training half of the men returned with tattoos, Matheny with two of them; one was a horned, blue Devil with a trident in his fist on one shoulder and on the other, a red heart with an arrow piercing it and "Mother" inscribed in the center of the heart. It all looked a little fantastic, what with his blonde hair cropped short, plethoric face and bulging biceps flexed for effect.

One evening Caanen lay on his bunk reading when Matheny suddenly stood beside his bed. "What are you, a pussy, Caanen? You didn't come with us for a beer. You Pussy!" Caanen groped for something to mollify him to avoid a fist pummeling. "Yea, I guess I am somewhat of a pussy," said Caanen feebly. Matheny scoffed and walked off.

Whaley told Paul that his response to Matheny was just right, "Why argue with the guy when you know good and well he can beat you to a pulp." However, Whaley's well-meaning statement did not ease the shame of allowing someone to threaten him.

Caanen knew that this was not how the pint-sized Private Maggio would have reacted to a bully in *From Here to Eternity*.

Eight weeks of grueling training finally ended. There was a sense of pride and a great deal of relief upon completing Boot Camp. Everyone anxiously awaited his next assignment. At the graduation ceremony each soldier learned of his next duty station. Whaley and Caanen drew Fort Ord, California the major jumping off point for infantrymen to Vietnam in 1965.

A MEXICAN INTERLUDE

Caanen was issued three weeks of leave prior to reporting to Fort Ord for Advanced Infantry Training. He went home where his mother was overjoyed to see her oldest son safe. His father who could not forgive him for his poor academic performance--Caanen had been suspended with failing grades from three universities—did not speak to him. His father was a Battalion Surgeon during World War II in France and Germany and refused to be drawn into any discussion about the military with Paul. He regarded Paul's entry into the military as a signal failure, whereas he (the father) had responded to his nation's call of duty. The evening TV news was preoccupied with Vietnam, a slow, agonizing process of disenchantment that culminated years later in withdrawal of forces from this sliver of a country.

Paul wandered tropical Mexico before beginning Advanced Training with a small haversack containing toilet items, a diary, *The Power and the Glory* by Graham Greene and *Plumed Serpent* by D.H. Lawrence. He left Mexico City on a second-class bus headed for the Yucatan. It was packed with people, poultry and goats. En route he saw the widest tree in the world, El Arbol del Tule in Santa Maria del Tule; he loitered in the cathedrals and ate his midday meals in the zocalos. He arrived one afternoon in Coatzacoalcos in a light rain that left a glistening sheen on the clay streets. He stepped off the bus near the zocalo and walked to the nearest hotel where he was the only lodger. Horsemen rode by slumped over in their ponchos, their horses' rumps slick with rainwater. Caanen caught a glimpse of the small harbor further down the roadway. He pulled on a poncho and walked under the covered sidewalk along the main street— saloon doors and windows were thrown open. Waitresses and bartenders sat around small round tables drinking and awaiting patrons. Caanen walked into one cavernous, empty saloon and ordered a beer, standing at the bar and looking at the reflection of the waterfront in the mirror behind the bar. Although he stayed for an hour, not one other customer arrived. Later in the evening he sat at the escritoire in his hotel room looking out the window, blurred with rivulets of rainwater. He wrote in his diary: "here in the jungle, everything is such a lonely endeavor—it must be very difficult to persevere with one's moral principles. I wonder if it will be the same in Vietnam." Maybe, he thought, he would fall apart like some of Greene's protagonists living in the tropics.

The following morning, he boarded the bus again, roughly following the path of the "whiskey priest" in *The Power and the Glory*. An older man sat across from Caanen holding on tightly to 4 turkeys whose heads protruded from a gunnysack. A middle-aged man with a handsome goatee settled down next to Caanen after swaying down the aisle.

He continued drinking from a bottle of tequila. Later, he was vomiting into the aisle. The bus arrived at Villahermosa late in the evening. Caanen pushed his way out of the crowded bus. The zocalo was alive with young children playing soccer and adolescent boys and girls parading around hand-in-hand. Their parents lay asleep on benches scattered about the adjoining streets. Caanen bought some pastry from a street vendor and retired to his hotel.

The next morning, he was on a wooden ferry near Frontera slowly travelling from an isthmus in the jungle to the mainland. Tall tropical trees lined the shoreline. The landing site was a short wooden pier. High rain clouds drifted by in the powdery blue noonday sky. The trees cast deep dark shadows on the water heightening the feeling of being surrounded by jungle.

By sunset he was in Oaxaca where he was accosted by a young man as he entered the foyer of Hotel Parador San Miguel.

"¿Habla espanol?," the young man said.

"Si, poquito," Caanen responded.

The lithe young man, the same height as Caanen, fell into excellent English, "I dance in the ensemble with the national troupe—you know, Folklorica Mejico. I'm heading home. How about sharing a room?" Caanen looked at him and agreed. The fellow had florid acne on the bridge of his nose but, dazzling white teeth.

The following morning the two walked to Monte Alban. On one of the immense mesas they rested and drank water.

"You don't sweat? Such perfect skin," the Mexican said. He was now speaking with a faint lisp. He began to search Paul's back for pimples. "I'll massage your neck."

"No, stop! Let's get back to exploring the site," said Caanen.

That night around two in the morning Caanen could feel his bed sheet being carefully removed. Then, a hand, ever so lightly, traveled up his thigh. He sat up abruptly.

"I would like to see what you have," said the young man.

"No! It's mine—get back in your bed!" Caanen shrieked. Like many a young man his age, sex was never far from Paul's mind. However, the actual act of sex was verboten. And with a man? Not even to be considered. He churned over the notion that night that he might be homosexual.

When Caanen arose, the young Mexican was gone. He boarded a bus for Chichen Itza and days later was on Isla de Mujeres, the only gringo on the island. Barracuda had migrated by the millions into the shallow waters around the island during the preceding month and there was nothing to do but wait for them to leave. All of the hotel rooms had emptied out. Caanen rented a hammock for 50 cents a night and wandered the island during the day. It was a lonely way to end a vacation.

He flew from Merida several days later to San Francisco where his father had reserved a room for him at the St. Francis Hotel. Although Paul and his father could not talk to one another, his father was a generous man. Paul sat in the lobby of the St. Francis on a richly embroidered damask covered lounge chair, smoking one cigarette after another, sipping coffee and reading *War and Peace*. It was ironic that Paul, now in love with the military, identified strongly with Pierre rather than the dashing, soon to Adjutant to General Kutusov, Prince Bolkonsky.

Early September was windy and cool in the Bay area and Paul was looking forward to Fort Ord. Military training featured physical endurance and Paul welcomed the challenge. Anything, anything to turn his mind from churning over and over about the Protestant, Midwestern fixations on sin, God or no God, and "making something" of one's self.

ADVANCED INFANTRY TRAINING

Caanen entered Fort Ord through West Gate flanked by tall dark spruce and monkey pines. The Pacific was visible behind rolling sand dunes covered by dry, brown bracken. Looking eastward he could see the silhouette of the Gabilan Mountain range.

The next morning at reveille thousands of young men lined up on the pavement in front of their barracks, sounding off while their platoon leaders took a head count. Shouts and whistles of Drill Sergeants echoed along the pavement between the buildings. Heavy clouds invested the coast in the early morning hours and towering spruces formed a barrier between company barracks; their tops occasionally sparkled with a rich viridian hue when the sun burst through the clouds. Advanced Infantry Training began much like Basic Training with soldiers waiting in line early in the morning. A cold fog lazily oozed along the low spots and in between the buildings. The line of men moved slowly into the armory where M-16s were issued to each trainee.

"Memorize the serial number on your piece—don't forget it," shouted the armory sergeant.

The damp, cold air bit through Caanen's fatigue jacket. Few recruits were accustomed to the cold of the California coast in fall. Later in the morning everyone was issued a jacket liner. The men marched back to their barrack past rows and rows of identical yellow wooden barracks that went on to infinity, falling out of sight only behind the rolling, hilly nature of the terrain. Shortly after the men returned to their barracks, they were ordered to shed their fatigue jackets and blouses and turn out in T-shirts for PT. There was never a moment to sit down or reflect on what was occurring; any free time was spent smoking cigarettes and complaining of having to "hurry up and wait".

Moving about in the fog reminded Caanen of a recurring boyhood dream wherein he commanded a platoon of men on the march to Vicksburg along the steamy, fog-bound Mississippi River. As a young child Caanen slept on the wooden floor of his bedroom for weeks on end hoping to prepare for West Point as Robert E. Lee is said to have done.

Dreams of military life had started early for Caanen but, by the time of being drafted his interests had drifted to philosophy and agriculture.

The Drill Sergeant's bedroom was on the first floor of the bi-level barrack across from the head. He was not as omnipresent as Sgt. Powell had been. He only infrequently addressed the men outside of formation and then, only at night when they were too tired to listen. He was neither as feared nor memorable as Powell. Everyone was asleep the moment lights out occurred at 10:00 PM.

Whaley sought out Caanen every moment he could. He wrote feverishly to his wife every day. She and the two children remained in Bridge City, Missouri waiting to hear where he would be stationed after Fort Ord. Fortunately, his small community helped care for his young family. He was convinced he would be assigned to Vietnam. Each day became agony for him.

The platoon went daily to the firing range for 4 hours of firing M-16s, 45-caliber pistols and 50-caliber machine guns at paper targets. Caanen and Whaley lay for hours on the firing line, the sun beating down on their metal helmets that became heavier as the afternoon wore on. Whaley was having difficulty hitting the near targets at 25 yards. One evening Whaley sat, slumped forward on the upper bunk after mail call holding an open letter from his wife in his hands. His eyes welled up with tears.

"I can't do this anymore," Whaley said. "I'm just no good in the Army—what am I gonna do in Nam?"

Caanen tried to cheer him up, pointing out the good things he had done like keeping out of trouble, keeping a neat footlocker, marching in step.

"Please…you know, and I know, that stuff's not important—I'm ashamed for my family. I'm not a warrior."

The live firing range was on the east side of the fort amongst pines and coastal oaks. The troops arrived at midday and disembarked from the transport trucks. The Mess Sergeant quickly prepared the food line. Caanen and Whaley smoked and waited their turn in the chow line.

Many of the men were anxious about the live ammo exercise, Whaley among them. Caanen tried to reassure him, "They'll be firing well above our heads—the nabobs don't want any trouble brought down on top of them because of some SNAFU."

The men seated themselves on wooden bleachers that formed an arc around a raised podium. An infantry captain turned on the microphone and began explaining the exercise. "Everyone will low crawl 300 yards under 50 caliber rounds fired at about waist level—there are explosives in bunkers along the way to simulate artillery and grenade explosions. Keep your head down—never, no matter what, stand up," said the captain.

A light rain began to fall and the troops broke out their ponchos. Suddenly there was a stuttering, crackling sound. Lightning temporarily blinded everyone as it struck a nearby utility pole. The microphone exploded in the captain's hand and he fell forward off the podium into the sand. After twenty minutes of confusion the officer was taken by helicopter to the base hospital. Another Range

Officer stepped into his place and continued explaining the drill. No further mention was made of the incident—did the officer recover? Or die? It was an ominous kick off for the live-fire range exercise.

Ninety minutes later the platoon was crawling under live fire. One soldier failed to make the crawl. He stopped and coiled up into the fetal position. He was removed by some of the trainers and was not seen in the barracks again. Whaley successfully completed the exercise and looked less troubled that evening in barracks.

One overnight exercise consisted of miles of walking and running through barren sectors of the fort. The men in the platoon were issued a compass and then abandoned on the crest of an immense knoll at sunset and told to navigate through "enemy territory" toward the objective: warehouses near a railroad spur, 12 miles away. Whaley stuck close to Caanen as the men dispersed from the dark coastal oaks on the side of hill. The halfmoon changed the landscape to a shimmering silver and grey. Caanen saw a pair of coyotes hunting on the slope of the hill, jogging from one shrub to another. The needle grass was waist high and obscured anyone who sat in it. By midnight Whaley and Caanen hiked 8 miles when they were suddenly set upon by 5 or 6 "enemy" troops. Whaley was grabbed from behind by one of the men, Caanen began running and leaping over low shrubs, jumping a dry creek bed. Two men chased him, but lost ground. They stopped, raised their rifles and fired blanks.

"Alright soldier, you're wounded now. Stop running," one of them shouted. "Hey asshole, you're s'posed to stop after shots are fired!"

Caanen outran the two pursuers and kept on in a slow jog. He didn't encounter anymore "enemy" and soon was in sight of the warehouses. He began creeping slowly toward the buildings. Suddenly his arms were forced behind his back and he was shoved to the ground.

"Hey, Hot Shot. You can't outrun us now," one of the pursuers said.

They forced Caanen to the ground in the prone position and strapped wires to his wrists and ankles that were attached to a car battery several feet away.

"Alright, let's see some pushups!" Caanen began doing pushups but felt a shudder and collapsed on his face. His nose began to bleed.

"Come on! Let's see some pushups, Hot Shot."

Caanen struggled for 15 minutes. Every time he pushed up, the electrical current was switched on and he collapsed to the ground. Later all the trainees were gathered up and trucked back to base. Those captured early in the evening were well rested and eager to have breakfast. Caanen tried to catch a few moments of uninterrupted sleep.

※

The afternoons were sunny and a good time for field training.

"Okay, listen up Assholes! This is one of the most important exercises you'll have. I know—I was in Nam for a year and could've used some of this training myself. Pay attention!" the Staff Sergeant shouted at the trainees.

The Sergeant drew the topography of the immediate area in the dust at his feet using a stick. "Look, we're gonna walk along this creek and attack the enemy at this point (making a circle in the dirt). The important thing to remember is that the enemy has artillery support and you'll need to use your training under fire to reach the objective. Caanen, take over as platoon leader."

"Yes Sir. Everyone lineup in two files behind me. Whaley, take Smith and go ahead of us to reconnoiter," said Caanen.

They had not proceeded fifty yards when there was a loud report from forward of their position. The Sergeant in charge of the exercise informed Caanen that there was an incoming round.

"Everyone hit the dirt," yelled Caanen.

After the first round exploded nearby the platoon ran toward the spot where the round exploded. This went on for several rounds before the entire platoon suddenly came under fire from the flank where the "enemy" rose up out of a creek bed. They had lain in the slow-moving water with just their faces above the surface. It was a complete surprise. Whaley and Smith looked crestfallen, having failed to recognize the danger.

"This is what Charlie will do. Remember it," said the sergeant. "You lead men have got to be on the lookout for anything and everything—there's a lot of water in Nam." Caanen reflected often on that exercise. It was a sobering demonstration of the vulnerability of the foot soldier in Vietnam.

∞

Caanen thought the world of a tall, thin Infantry Major with handlebar moustaches whom he encountered around Headquarters—it was rumored this man had served two tours in Vietnam and been injured. Although Caanen did not talk to him, he envied the man's reputation and appearance. Caanen learned that his scores on the Army entrance tests were high enough to be eligible for officers training. He called his father informing him of his goal of becoming a career officer.

"Why? This will obligate you to stay longer in the service. Are you so taken by this popinjay Major and his moustaches? That's a foolish reason to make a choice like that. I would advise you to get out as soon as you can," his father implored him. Caanen notified HQ staff the following day that he wanted to attend Officers Candidate School. His father was correct. He was lost for things to do in life and now was bewitched by dreams of a glorious career in the military.

Days later a large assembly of men were addressed by their officers who informed them of their next station. Privates Caanen and Hyland would be going to Artillery Officers Candidate School. The others, including Whaley, were assigned to ship out for Vietnam. Days later, Caanen said goodbye to a troubled Whaley, now resigned to his fate and boarding a bus for Los Angeles. Hyland and Caanen remained at Ft. Ord until a new OCS class began at Ft. Sill, Oklahoma months later.

THE FEMALE PFC

"Sergeant Rogers wants you at headquarters in five minutes, Private." Caanen jogged down the macadam past the row of barracks to Headquarters office. He scattered a small flock of Brewer's blackbirds walking alongside him on the pavement with their quirky head movements. They were common on the fort in fall and winter. He rapped on the door with his knuckles, "Here to see Sergeant Rogers," Caanen said, coming to attention. He was tanned and more muscular after months of training, his hair closely cropped.

An attractive brunette woman, PFC with ample breasts looked over her glasses toward him and smiled in a knowing fashion, "He'll be with you in a minute Private. Stand at ease."

First Sergeant Rogers walked out from his small office and leaned on the counter with his elbows. He was ruggedly good looking, deeply tanned, his face creased from smoking and outdoor exposure. He cadged a cigarette from the smiling PFC who shook the pack toward him, the cigarette protruding from the pack.

Rogers lit up and said, "I gotta an order here says you and Hyland are going to OCS at Fort Sill. You lucky bastards! In the meantime, you're going to train our recruits to march. They're all headed for Nam." The young PFC came up behind Rogers and pressed her breasts against his back and smiled. Sergeant Rogers smiled.

"Sgt. Stringer, come over here," said Rogers. A small, very fat and dumpily dressed Staff Sergeant stepped forward from a chair behind the door. His helmet lacked the shine of the regular Drill Sergeant. It was smudged with fingerprints.

"I want you to see that Hyland and Caanen lack for nothing to get these recruits trained."

"Yes Sarge. Wilco," said Stringer in a falsetto voice.

"Stringer! It is not Sarge. Its "Top" or First Sergeant! Git the Hell out of here!" Rogers said.

"Yes sir, First Sergeant!" shouted Stringer.

The following morning Hyland and Caanen took their squads out on the pavement in front of the barracks. By this time both of them had sewn corporal's chevrons on their shoulders. The sky was locked under dishwater grey cloud and the fog was cold and thick.

Caanen trained his men strictly by the manual demonstrating commands to them and then having them mimic the movements. The training went slowly—several men never could remember to turn to their left or to keep in step. Hyland, on the other hand, befriended his men and had them skipping in unison to the amazement and derision of onlookers. Caanen heard Hyland's men laughing and enjoying themselves. He felt a flush of jealousy in his neck and jaw. It was obvious Hyland's platoon was learning to march quicker than his own men. Caanen felt Hyland was currying the favor of his men, rather than leading by example.

"Don't be so stiff, Caanen. Get into the rhythm of it. You're too military. Show some innovation," Hyland said to Caanen later in the day as the two retired to their quarters. Hyland had been drafted into the Army as Caanen had, but he regarded it as an imposition and resented his current status whereas, Caanen envisioned an illustrious military career in store for himself. Hyland had attended Indiana University for 4 semesters, dropped out to "take stock of his life" and was summarily drafted like Caanen.

Hyland and Caanen worked diligently over the next several months to get their men ready for the parade ground. First Sgt. Rogers called them to Headquarters on short notice one day. The young brunette PFC, as was customary, walked up to the counter and pressed her breasts against Rogers' back. She stared fixedly at the two corporals without a change in her expression.

"Good job! Your barracks look really sharp. All your men will be shipping out for Vietnam in two weeks," Rogers said. He could see the two young corporals were looking at the PFC. Rogers smiled and dismissed them. The sexual overtone in Headquarters was a stark difference from the barracks where men were too tired to even dream of sex.

To celebrate his success in training, Caanen took a weekend leave to visit Monterey. He stayed overnight in a rundown hotel two blocks from the bay and ate all his meals at the wharf. He bought several packs of Players "Navy Cut" cigarettes with orange tobacco wrapped in thin paper in an aluminum foil-lined box. The box had a multicolored painting of a shoreline with a lighthouse and a bearded seaman in the center of a ring buoy. Caanen felt sophisticated as he carefully removed a cigarette and lighted it. He walked into the city center and thumbed through used books in an old bookstore across the street from the abandoned laboratory of Ed Ricketts, Steinbeck's great friend. Robinson Jeffers, some beat poets and Henry Miller were the mainstays on the shelves. Caanen worked his way over to the abandoned canneries and forced his way into one of the buildings. The dilapidated building was a large cavernous metal shed, perhaps 4 stories high. Small engine motors lay about on the wooden plank floor; oil still leaking from around the engine gaskets and spreading across the floor. Metal sheets lining the walls were loose and folded back on themselves. Through the gaps Caanen could see miles out to a glorious sea, bathed in light. He walked down the rusted, grated steps to the water level below.

Barnacles covered the concrete pylons supporting the tar-streaked wooden fretwork. The water was ominously dark. He clambered back up onto the main floor where he found an old yellowed copy of the Monterey Peninsula *Herald* lying on a wooden platform. In it a Want Ad from August 15, 1954 began: "homing pigeons and milk goats for sale at homestead, route 3, box 202." A totally different era, ancient history he thought, dropping the paper and leaving the building. Forty years in the future he would experience a similar feeling about this very moment, "ancient history" he would say. Gulls shrieked overhead. Caanen warmed himself by leaning against the sunbaked corrugated iron siding of the cannery and looked out to sea. Sunlight flashed into his eyes.

TELL ME ALL ABOUT IT

Sgt. Stringer took a strong liking to the two young men, showing Hyland and Caanen how to inspect the barracks to uncover the many tricks recruits employed to get out of cleaning the building properly. Stringer's conversation never strayed far from worrying about his future in the Army. He had married a Korean woman and had two children. Bad evaluations by supervisors at his last two duty stations dogged him and he couldn't afford another. Beneath the helmet liner a spike of oily black hair showed. He had a small, red, pimply nose. There was little that was military about him.

Caanen mentioned that he hoped to soon be an officer. Stringer was saddened by this revelation because Caanen would not be around long enough to help him and listen to his fears. The two men visited Stringer's home in the married housing section on base. Two small raven-haired boys pounced on their father. His wife was diffident and timid.

"I wish I could be stationed in Korea again. I liked it there," said Stringer. "Maybe you could put in a good word for me with First Sergeant Rogers. He's always chewing me out about my dress. I gotta have a good evaluation." Stringer's wife smiled kindly at Caanen and Hyland. Caanen was sympathetic to Stringer's plight, but knew he was powerless to help him.

After the recent batch of Advanced Training recruits embarked for Vietnam, Caanen was assigned as a guard at the base Court and

Hyland left for another training assignment. Caanen arrived at court daily with a loaded .45 caliber pistol and reported to a weary Captain in the Adjutant Corps who chain-smoked from behind his desk while sitting in a wooden swivel chair. His dark hair was disheveled.

"Light up if you want, Corporal. We're going to get to know one another well in the next month. All you need to do here is bring in the prisoners and have them stand in front of me. You stand off to the side over there. Remember your piece is loaded for a reason. Some of these bastards are nuttier than shit. You're here to protect me. Everyone one of these SOB's is a deserter and should be put away for years."

The first day set the tone for the remainder of the month. Caanen went to the large reception room crowded with young men in civilian clothes. Some of them were in rags.

He called out, "Jeff Taylor, come with me."

A tall dark-haired man of twenty-five came up to Caanen. He wore a ponytail and his face was covered with beard. He was wearing a dirty T-shirt and jeans with holes in the knees. Caanen led him before the Captain.

"Pfc Jeffrey Taylor?"

"Yes sir."

"I see where you went AWOL over a year ago from Ft. Ord and were recently captured by the Sherriff's patrol in Salinas."

"Well, I wasn't AWOL sir. I had a pass and then I had a bit of a mental breakdown."

"Oh, really?"

"Yes sir. You can see by my paperwork that I should've been given a medical discharge. It just isn't fair for someone who suffered like I have."

"Oh, tell me about it," said the Captain leaning back and lighting a cigarette. He smirked at Caanen as if to say, 'let's hear all about it.'

"Well sir, I was doing well in my unit earning a pass to San Francisco and then all shit broke loose. I fell in love with sheep sir. I've been living with them since—I have sex with them constantly." Taylor delivered these statements with perfect sangfroid. The captain was waiting for him to smile or trip up in some way.

"You know you're the third guy who has come here with the exact same story this week. You ain't getting out of this man's Army for bestiality because frankly I don't believe you. Furthermore, you're not going to get a Section 8 for this. Now get out!"

"But sir. Please, I'm sick, too sick to go on."

"Bullshit! Now get him out of here!"

Caanen witnessed similar and just as improbable, if not identical explanations by dozens of deserters during the following days. The captain was weary of listening to the lies and excuses of the men brought in for questioning.

Sergeant Stringer often came to Caanen's barracks just to chat. As usual he was worried about his longevity in the service. "I'd git out, but what would I do to support my children and wife." He sat on the bunk opposite Caanen haplessly twirling his helmet liner in circles as he spoke. He loved his family and was genuinely distressed that he could not find his way in the Army. His dark hair was oily and unkempt, his bulbous nose and cheeks were inflamed with rosacea—Caanen felt hopeless as well listening to the story. Stringer got into his Ford pickup and drove back to the married quarters after running out of things to talk about. Sgt. Stringer coming to some good end seemed very improbable indeed. Caanen was to command another sergeant within a year who married a poor Asian woman and had children—it was not an unusual solution for some socially misfit men.

One joke making the rounds captured the zaniness of men trying to get out of the service: "A recruit walks up to the main gate with his arms outstretched as if driving a motorcycle. He makes the sounds of a motorcycle, twisting his right wrist as if he were gunning the throttle. He asks the main gate guard, "Can I go out now?" The guard says, "No" and orders him to return to the fort. He repeats this process over and over, being refused each time at the gate until he is finally reported to the base psychiatrist. A week later he 'rides his motorcycle' to the main gate, hands the guard his Medical Discharge Form, lifts his right leg from over the make-believe motorcycle, turns off the engine and turns to the guard, "Here, I don't need these keys anymore. You can have the bike. I got my Section 8."

NIETZSCHE

A month later Caanen was in Ft. Sill, Oklahoma attending Artillery Officers Candidate School (OCS) with 110 other candidates in a training company spread over two barracks. They would be there for the next six months. The fresh candidates mustered on the parade ground in the morning. The captain in charge of the class greeted them with derision.

"You're gonna need to look sharper than this tomorrow. Stand up there, Candidate!"

A tall shambling fellow by the name of Gilroy stood as erect as he could, still leaning out over his feet.

"We're going to issue you everything you'll need for the next six months. You'll want nothing but guts!"

By the end of the first week over a dozen candidates quit. The pace was torrid: up at 5:00 AM, calisthenics and then double-time to classes. Formations, and more formations, accompanied with verbal harangues from the supervising officers. Lights out was at 10:00 PM.

Supervising officers stepped into the barracks each morning and struck the top of a garbage can with a metal rod to awaken the men. Everyone shot out of bed and collided with one another reaching for their shoes and trousers. If, in the opinion of the officers, the previous day had not gone well everyone was ordered to grasp their footlocker and carry it out to the parade ground on their head and begin a one-mile jog around the track, return to barracks to shower, fall out again and begin calisthenics.

Hyland bunked in a different barrack than Caanen. He walked alongside Caanen to the mess hall for breakfast one morning. "'I don't know that I can do this much longer," said Hyland, "'No price is too high to pay for the privilege of owning yourself' as Nietzsche said."

"Stick it out Hyland! This isn't about German philosophical ideas! You've already shown you can lead men. Stick it out man. Your hero Nietzsche even treasured his military service," said Caanen.

There were three types of officer candidates in the company: college graduates, college dropouts and former non-commissioned officers. Few men were college graduates, the vast number of candidates being dyed-in-the-wool Army men, ambitious non-coms hoping to trade up to become junior officers. These men were older than the others with clear goals in mind and often with a family behind them. They rarely mixed with candidates Caanen's age. The college dropouts were the least distinguished of the three groups, but the closest knit. Caanen fit nicely in this group having failed out of 3 universities.

Caanen ran into Hyland in the third week of OCS just before morning calisthenics. Hyland's jaw was set.

"I've had enough of this. I'm no longer willing to be a cipher!" he said looking into Caanen's eyes. The following day Hyland was absent from the morning formation. That weekend Caanen saw him with other soldiers who had 'fallen from grace.' Washed out from OCS, they were policing the grounds for cigarette butts and scraps of paper thrown between the barracks.

"I think they're going to ship us off to Nam as soon as possible," Hyland said to Caanen. "My parents will be heartbroken. I don't think they'll understand." Caanen could not fully comprehend why Hyland allowed himself to be sent off to Vietnam in such a reckless fashion—it seemed riskier than the apathy that had landed Caanen in the military.

Lehrer was another college dropout whom Caanen befriended and the two crossed paths infrequently, usually during body hygiene drills at night while showering or brushing their teeth. Lehrer was handy with historical references. He was also over six feet tall with dark hair and thick glasses.

"We've got to finish this training strong. Like Xenophon going into Persia, we've got to come out at some point. By the way, I saw Hyland doing KP for the chow hall. He's still waiting for orders for Nam," he said.

Caanen felt a twinge of regret at the mention of his fellow drill corporal at Fort Ord. "Maybe I'm not as principled as he," Caanen thought to himself.

PACINNI

Caanen enjoyed the verbal to-and-fro with the Supervising Captain during calisthenics. His joking around often led to more exercises for all the candidates. Many candidates showed their displeasure. "It's okay if you want to do the exercises, just don't make us pay for it," he was told by one older candidate. On weekends candidates spent time preparing their gear for the upcoming week and studying artillery manuals. Those who accrued twenty or more demerits over the prior week were forced to "jark"—a 12-mile forced march uphill with a pack conducted in the afternoon when temperatures often reached 100 degrees Fahrenheit. Caanen spent every Saturday "jarking" as payment for his bantering during calisthenics. Gilroy was the only other candidate who jarked as often as Caanen, but his demerits were accumulated for sloppiness. An ambulance followed the men up to the crest of the hill six miles out from the barracks and followed them home. Often Gilroy could be seen feigning physical exhaustion and hitching a ride back to the barracks, his tall, lean frame hunched over the tailgate of ¼ ton truck with legs dangling.

Fortunately, Caanen's conduct in the classroom was exceptional, particularly in artillery survey that consisted of applied algebra and trigonometry. He also excelled in close order drill, which was rote memorization of commands and movements while marching. He was so good at calling out the instructions for close order drill he began to think of himself as the *idiot savant*, Lieutenant Scheiskopf, of *Catch 22* fame.

Neither Lehrer nor Caanen saw Hyland again. He disappeared from KP service, silently, stealthily shipped off to Vietnam.

A small satellite of men began to gather several yards away from the main formation of candidates each morning. This was the sick call list. Normally, it required a serious injury to make the list, usually to the feet—sprained ankles, infections or broken bones. The men reported to the hospital daily and traveled by van to their classes. Candidate Pacinni began to join sick call each morning.

"Candidate Pacinni you're on sick call again?" the Captain shouted.

"Yes, Sir! I am Sir!" Pacinni was short and stumpy with a Jersey accent. The other candidates were skeptical of his injury. Pacinni was unfazed by the innuendos. A jeep drove the injured man to the classrooms. Pacinni was always waiting at the entrance to the classrooms when the remainder of the company arrived by foot later.

"How in the hell do you do it, Pacinni?" Lehrer asked.

"What d'ya mean," Pacinni responded.

"I mean you haven't marched to class in a month. What the hell is the matter with you anyway?"

"I've got some sort of foot problem. Anyway, I'm not supposed to run on it." Pacinni's explanation wasn't very convincing.

Every morning the footlockers stationed at the end of each bed were opened for inspection while the candidates were eating breakfast. An extra pair of boots was set alongside the footlocker. Caanen often returned from the chow hall to find his footlocker overturned because of inadequately polished boots or improperly folded underwear. Pacinni's footlocker was always wide open and untouched. He paid other candidates to shine his boots, tend to his footlocker and buy extra time in the shower at night. Still, he mustered in with sick call each morning.

Classroom work was continued eight hours a day and the candidates had difficulty staying awake, particularly in the hot Quonset huts used as classrooms. One candidate each week was the 'commander" for the other hundred men. The candidates were always accompanied by commissioned officers whose job was to evaluate the leadership quality of the "commander."

WEEKEND IN LAWTON

One Friday afternoon candidates were given leave for the weekend. Pacinni and Caanen stood at the main gate in uniform waiting for a taxi to take them to town.

"You got a hot date, Caanen?" Pacinni asked.

"No, I'm going to the movies," Caanen said.

"Come with me, I've got a better idea."

Caanen agreed, not having anything planned but uncertain as to what Pacinni had in mind.

The two jumped out of the taxi in downtown Lawton and entered the Lawtonian Hotel. The reception counter was manned by a fellow with slick, oily black hair who was busy smoking and inhaling to his toes. There was a byzantine network of pigeonholes behind him where keys were placed.

"Can I talk to the bellhop," Pacinni said, matter of factly.

"He's upstairs, wait for him in the foyer," the desk clerk said picking up his cigarette from the square glass ashtray.

Caanen and Pacinni slumped into separate beat-up leather divans.

A medium-sized black man with pencil thin moustaches and a wasp-like waist approached the seated men, "O.K. let's go," he said walking to the elevator.

They went up to the 10th floor, walked to the fire escape at the end of the hallway and then carefully walked down the grated steps clinging to the side of the hotel. The three reentered the hotel on the 5th floor. The bellhop tapped on the door of room 512.

"Come in," said a soft voice.

Caanen and Pacinni walked into the room, the bellhop followed. A thirty-ish, attractive blonde with a lithe figure and only a modest amount of makeup sat on the bed fidgeting with a pocket mirror and tweezers.

"Hi Gregory, how are you?"

"I'm fine Ma'am. Brought you two."

"You guys lookin" for some excitement?" she said glancing at Pacinni and Caanen.

"Maybe," said Pacinni.

"Twenty for a blow job and thirty for 'around the world."

Caanen lost all sexual curiosity after her crude statement. He was intimidated by her forthrightness regarding the act of sex. Pacinni abruptly turned and headed for the door, "Let's see the next one, Sport," he said out of the corner of his mouth to Gregory.

The three men looked into no less than five different rooms. Pacinni wasn't satisfied.

"This is not for us Chief!" he said.

Gregory, the bellhop, lit a cigarette and exhaled, staring at the two men. They returned to the foyer and then out on to the darkened street where Pacinni hailed a cab. Caanen got in behind Pacinni.

The cab headed for the black section of town. The taxi stopped on a tree-lined, ill-lit street. Pacinni got out and walked to a small bungalow. Fifteen minutes later he resurfaced and walked to the cab.

"I'm staying here, Caanen. See ya tomorrow."

Caanen took the cab back to the base.

"WHO DO YOU THINK YOU ARE?"

Temperatures soared above 100^0 F. almost daily. Jarks became nearly impossible in the oppressive heat, lasting an hour longer than usual because the pace was so slow. Fewer and fewer jarkers were able to complete the entire run—picked up by the ambulance that trailed behind. Caanen began to rethink his demeanor in calisthenics—his responses of "Yea" and "Nope" became "Yes, Sir" and "No, Sir" in order to reduce his demerits and avoid the Jark.

Caanen served as the Commander of candidates for one week. He marched the candidates to and from class, provided daily bulletins and occasionally corrected mistakes of other candidates. Caanen attempted to explain why the orders were as they were. The men responded to his unusual leadership. The supervising officers thought him promising. Some of the easy-going, laissez faire philosophy of the benighted Pfc. Hyland had rubbed off on him. He was more insightful and empathic when addressing the company of fellow trainees than other candidate leaders had been. The older candidates, when appointed temporary commanders, lost their tempers, blamed their classmates for any mistakes made and chewed-out their fellow candidates, generally behaving as if they already had their commission. Caanen treated the other candidates as equal partners rather than subordinates resulting in a modest improvement of morale.

Leave was no longer granted on weekends, as there was an urgency to get trainees out of school and off to Vietnam. Officers were short-lived in Vietnam, particularly artillery officers who served as forward observers. It was said that once fire was called in on an enemy site, the half-life of the forward observer who ordered the strike was measured in minutes. The North Vietnamese were extremely proficient in returning counter fire.

Graduation finally arrived. Caanen's family drove to Lawton for the weekend. Caanen stood on stage, one of five honor graduates, all of whom were offered permanent positions in the Armed Forces. The recipients were assured of never being 'riffed' by the Army, the same honor accorded officers who graduated from West Point. However, it came with an obligation of more years in service. Here was the ticket to a glorious beginning as an officer, however, Caanen had grown increasingly skeptical of life in the Army. The daily repetition of menial tasks had become onerous and he could not foresee being told what to do all day long, every day. He declined the offer of a permanent officer position and the award was immediately seized upon by the candidate next in line, a former sergeant first class in the Army Engineer Corps. The older man could not understand why Caanen turned down the offer and resented the younger man, interpreting Caanen's refusal as an insult to the service. Caanen's parents drove him home for several days leave after the ceremony. His mother and even his father were proud of him graduating with honors. His father even softened his objections to the Army after learning Caanen had turned down the offer of permanent employment.

Caanen and Lehrer received orders to stay at Fort Sill and attend Artillery Survey School. They moved to officers' quarters that resembled a college dormitory.

Classes commenced the following Monday. Caanen settled into a small student desk. The courses were applied mathematics taught by a dry, disinterested officer faculty. The teachers appeared too untidy to be career soldiers. Caanen was quick to answer questions and gained the attention of the instructor. However, he reverted back to his old college habits of reading into the early morning hours and arriving late for class. After the third infraction, the captain teaching the class called him forward.

"Do you have a doctor's slip to explain the tardiness?" "No, Sir."

"I didn't think so! You're to report to the Base Commander tomorrow! Eight o'clock sharp!"

Caanen arrived thirty minutes early for the appointment. He waited in the general's anteroom until a Major ordered him into the Base Commander's office. He walked to within two paces of the large desk, stood at attention and saluted,

"Second Lieutenant Caanen, reporting Sir!"

The general was meticulously coiffed and without a wrinkle in his clothing. His forearms rested on the large desktop, palms down.

"Why were you late for class?" The Brigadier left the younger officer standing at attention.

"I was reading Sir!"

"You were, *what*?"

"I was reading late, Sir."

"*What* were you reading?"

"A novel, Sir, *"Barbary Shore."*

"*What* kind of crap is this? *Who* do you think you are? I'll ship you to Nam right now if you're late by so much as a minute from now on. Furthermore, you'll be private Caanen. Do you understand?"

"Yes, Sir!"

"Get out! I don't want to see you in here again."

Caanen was never late again in the Army. The General meant what he said. It was the first time Caanen had encountered an authority (in college, at home, or in the military) who meant precisely what he said. Caanen could not manipulate the general as he had his high school and college teachers who succumbed to clever, intellectual banter.

The survey course was tedious. Field exercises were conducted on the hilly part of the fort where the students experienced all aspects of surveying: calculating elevation, measuring distance, and computing longitude and latitude, and the distance the artillery round travelled to target. The weather was often cold and foggy in the mornings but, warmed during the day and the oak strewn hillsides began to change colors in the Indian summer. The trainees trooped over the hillsides with theodolites and distance measuring tapes and scopes. A short lunch break on a sunny hillside was their reward for clambering over the inaccessible topography.

Following graduation from survey school, the officers were handed their new orders with future destinations. A "benevolent hand" interceded for Caanen once again, sparing him from Vietnam. Caanen was ordered to the Republic of Korea. Lt. Lehrer was to go to Camp Lewis, Washington for further schooling in Motor Pool operation and then to join Caanen in Korea. The remainder of the officers embarked for Vietnam.

PREFACE TO BOOK II

"...US imperialists should...
be bound hand and foot everywhere they are..."
Speech to Korean Workers party
by Kim Il Sung, October 5, 1966

By 1966 South Korea was an 18-year old republic ruled by authoritarian Park Chung He. Along with his cronies, Park established himself in the presidential palace following a *coup d' etat* in 1961. His Communist adversary across the DMZ, Kim Il-Sung concocted a brand of guerilla warfare to try and destabilize his southern neighbor. This methodology continued until late 1968.

The Republic of Korea was rural; the vast majority of 31 million inhabitants lived in isolated, small villages, without electricity and running water. The country is roughly the size of Kentucky and transportation other than by foot was by Kim chi bus, a small box-shaped vehicle capable of carrying ten or twelve passengers.

There were 55,000 US soldiers and a sprinkling of Thai, Turk and other international soldiers under the command of the one-eyed patrician, 4-star general, Charles H. Bonesteel. In 1967 these soldiers were complemented with a number of "McNamara Specials," part of Project 100,000 that sent mentally and medically enfeebled men off to serve in Korea and Vietnam. The 'Moron Corps' were a hazard not for the enemy, but their own compatriots.

BOOK II

Life Near the DMZ, First Year (1966)

SANTA BARBARA

Army personnel in dress greens boarded the Northwest 747 in a light, cold rain. They were to fly from Seattle to Kimpo Airport, Seoul, Korea. Caanen sat in the rear of the plane. The stewardess served him coffee as he looked out the starboard window at the Aleutians below. Suddenly the wing swayed up and down. Caanen was alarmed. He recalled the stewardess and pointed toward the undulating wing.

"That's normal. They're made to do that," she said, smiling broadly. The enlisted men seated around Caanen snickered, happy to catch out the greenhorn lieutenant.

The aircraft landed in Seoul in the early morning hours of a moonless night in utter darkness. The men deplaned and were bussed to a nearby military base. A bitterly cold, steel-gray dawn unfolded. Mothers and children walked along the roadway, their children in black school uniforms and caps pulled down around their ears. Several youngsters skated on frozen rice paddies carefully avoiding the few rice straw clumps protruding above the ice surface. Light snow drifted across the pavement and swirled on the ice with each gust of wind. One boy skated recklessly fast, unfazed, leaning forward over his skates and tugging on his cap.

Later that day Caanen boarded a light prop plane and flew to a support base near the DMZ. He entered the Quartermaster hut and drew winter clothing: woolen shirts and trousers, long underwear and a parka. Waiting in line for his clothing he overheard a loudspeaker on the other side of the DMZ, "Ru-tenent Canine, Ru-tenent Canine happy you fly here. Come over here, join your true comrades."

The sergeant handed him his gear and said, "Don't worry about that. That's old Charlie, he knew you were coming for weeks. Somehow they get hold of our rosters and do that to every new officer that flies in here. Makes you feel secure, huh?"

The next day Caanen loaded his duffle bag into a helicopter and was flown to I Corps Headquarters just below the DMZ at Camp Santa Barbara, named after the patron saint of artillery. It was the hub of all artillery operations in the country.

"It's gonna to be rough up here," the helicopter pilot said, shouting over the racket of the blades, "you'll see, you're gonna freeze your ass off. This is the 'land of the frozen Chosun.' Where you from in the States, anyway?"

"Kansas."

"Me, I'm from Florida. This is not my idea of a resort."

The chopper set down on the helipad surrounded by tall Korean pines and granite boulders. Caanen thought it similar to the Canadian wilderness.

He dragged his gear to Headquarters where a large diagram of the chain of command hung on the wall. There were two photographs on the chart, one of President Johnson and the other of the Eighth Army commander, Bonesteel. Below these two men was the name of the I Corps commander.

The Headquarters clerk looked up from his log. Caanen detected an ironic smile. "Morning, Sir. The General is expecting you, Sir."

"Second Lieutenant Caanen reporting for duty, Sir!"

Caanen stood at attention and saluted. The Brigadier General looked up, he was a man in his late forties, lean, wiry, graying, clean-shaven and severe.

"Stand easy, son," he said. "I personally like to meet every officer we have in I Corps. You will be heading out to my old artillery unit, the 1st of the 17th. They're right below the DMZ. Here in Korea it is different from home..." he shifted in the swivel chair, "the temptations are great, but I expect all my officers to conduct themselves in a moral fashion and above reproach. Are you married, son?"

"No, Sir."

The general leaned forward on his desktop with his elbows, pressing his fingers together making a small steeple. "This is an impoverished land and many of the Korean girls have turned to prostitution. I have rules about officers going out with women over here"—the general continued, brushing some imaginary lint off the desktop. "It's simply not going to happen. There is no innocent conversation between you and a Korean girl. You'll be finished in this man's Army if you're caught out with any native girls. Stay in your officer's club and out of the village! Colonel Fitzpatrick who is the commander of the 1st of the 17th believes even stronger than I do in this approach. We're going to straighten this command up."

The Headquarters clerk looked up, arched his eyebrow, pursed his lips and raised his chin knowingly as Caanen walked out of the general's office.

Caanen bunked that evening in a Quonset hut with several officers who had been stationed at I Corps for months. A junior officer from the quartermaster section offered him a beer from the refrigerator. They sat down in a small area that served as a living room complete with a couch and several easy chairs. The talk soon shifted to the general's "morality play."

"That guy is obsessed with sex, I'm telling ya. Didn't he threaten you about talking to Korean girls? No one pays any attention to him in the entire country, you'll see. Oh, here's Park. Set up the dartboard would ya, Park?"

The small, dark, shiny haired man shook his head from side to side and disappeared into the bowels of the Quonset hut. He returned with a dartboard and a handful of steel-pointed darts with brightly colored fletching. Three other junior officers soon joined in, sipping beer, smoking cigarettes and throwing darts. Suddenly there was a loud thud as a captain burst through the front door, kicking it open. He was holding an armful of shotguns.

"Park! Beers all around," he shouted. "Newcomer, huh?" he said looking at Caanen.

The captain's factotum (surname also 'Park', as common as Smith in the States) followed him with a wooden box laden with ring-necked pheasants.

"That's got to be over the limit."

"There ain't any limit in this God-forsaken place," said the captain. Medical Corps officers generally didn't believe Army rules applied to them. The Captain was already a little drunk. He had driven the jeep back to the base with his houseboy sitting in the rear of the jeep cradling the game birds and handing cans of beer forward.

An hour later the junior officers were still drinking and playing darts. The captain ordered his houseboy to stand against the wall with his arms outstretched.

"Alright, the rules are that you pay Park 5 bucks every time you hit him with a dart. Closest dart wins the round."

"Five dolla," Park said showing his yellowing teeth.

Caanen looked at the captain dubiously. "Count me out," he said and went to look for his bunk.

The following morning Caanen walked to the Santa Barbara Officers Club for breakfast. The other officers were still very much asleep or hung over. The limestone block building had heavy, dark wooden shingles. Massive roughly hewn wooden beams framed the entrance to the dining room. Caanen looked out a large plate glass window onto a rampaging torrent below. The sides of the chasm were granite boulders overtopped by large pines. Water surged over the smooth-shouldered stones. None of the tumult of the waters could be heard from within.

ARRIVING AT 1/17TH FIELD ARTILLERY

Caanen flew from I Corps in a single engine plane later in the morning and reported for duty at Camp McIntyre, home of the 1st of the 17th, a fully tracked 8-inch howitzer battalion. This weapon was the pride of the artillery, capable of firing one shot on top of another, into the same impact hole from 14,000 meters away. The Headquarters encampment was surrounded by ten-foot high woven wire encased with concertina wire at its base and top. Uniformed civilian police walked the perimeter. The battalion Headquarters building was located near the fort's front gate at the base of a very large valley, flanked on each side with barren hillsides stripped of all vegetation large enough to burn. He unpacked his gear in a Quonset hut (fondly known as a hooch), which he shared with another recent arrival, 2nd Lieutenant William Schuette. The hut was placed on a concrete slab adjacent to several other huts, all perched on a steep hillside.

Headquarters lay below them. Two Quonset huts loomed high above his hooch that belonged to the Battalion Commander and Battalion Executive Officer, respectively.

Caanen entered HQ and waited twenty minutes to meet the Battalion XO. Major Roscoe Wilson burst through a door nearby. Caanen leaped to his feet and stood at attention.

"Good morning, Sir."

"At ease, Lieutenant. Come on into my office."

Major Wilson was a tall, thin, slightly stooped black man. His nose was aquiline and his skin, a light coffee color. The best adjective to describe him was elegant but, with a touch of weariness, perhaps from living in Korea for a year and dealing with the endless difficulties of junior officers. He was excited about welcoming new officers to the battalion.

"I'm sure you've received the Brig's warning about women up at Corps Headquarters. That goes ditto for down here. Colonel Fitzpatrick is cut out of the same cloth as the general. Just don't go taking off for the 'ville'," Wilson said.

All this talk of native women was beginning to have the opposite effect to that intended, at least upon Caanen. He knew nothing of Korean women when he arrived and had not given them a thought. Korean women seemed to be an obsession of the brass. The topic of women seemed incongruous here near the DMZ, the only women Caanen had seen were farmers' wives walking along the roadside, asexual and elderly.

"You'll be XO for Headquarters Battery, Caanen. Reeves is the Battery Commander and has lots of military experience, so this should let you settle in nicely," Wilson continued. His office was sprinkled with photographs of his children and wife. There were no weapons or any tokens to suggest that one was dealing with a warrior rather than a bank president.

Later in the morning Caanen walked into his new office, the Headquarters Battery Orderly Room. He was greeted by First Sergeant Williams, Corporal Clark, the battery clerk and 1st Lieutenant Reeves. Reeves lit a cigarette with his Zippo lighter and looked up at his new XO.

"I'm Ed Reeves. Welcome aboard." He reached out his hand to Caanen.

"Morning, Sir," said Williams and Clark in one voice.

"I expect you'll be wanting to know what to do here," said Reeves. He was a young man, twenty-four or twenty-five years of age, but looked older. He was shorter than Caanen, wiry in build with a light complexion, reddish hair and angular facial bones.

"I've been here six months and can't wait to go home," Reeves said exhaling smoke slowly. I see you came out of OCS, so did I. I used to be a tech sergeant in Transportation before I went to OCS.

Reeves looked out the front window of the Quonset hut at a group of men loitering about. He said, "Go out there and straighten out that formation. They need their dress squared away." Reeves had served as an enlisted man for five years and was hypercritical of the turnout of the men. He daily inspected their clothes, boots and gloves, a habit strongly approved by First Sgt. Williams.

Caanen embarked on his new task. He made sure the enlisted men were dressed correctly and quizzed them on the Chain of Command.

"Alright soldier, who is the Eighth Army Commander?" shouted Caanen.

"General Bonesteel, Sir!" the private shouted.

"Who is the I Corps Commander, private?"

The Chain of Command was a favorite topic. A large billboard was posted at every entrance to Armed Forces units in Korea—a wooden sign 10 feet in length and 4 feet in height with Bonesteel's name at the top and separate slabs of wood (removable) for lesser officers' names, tracing the lineage from Bonesteel to the battalion level.

In reality, General Bonesteel was remote from the work-a-day routine of Army life. He wore a chic black patch on his left eye that reminded Caanen of James Joyce, even to such details as the eye patch being on the same eye. By all accounts however, the general did a creditable job dealing with the unpredictable North Koreans.

FIELD EXERCISE

The Officers Club was halfway up the hillside and built of limestone on a theme similar to the building in Santa Barbara. A bronze battalion insignia hung over the entrance. Several juniper shrubs huddled alongside the walkway. Inside was a large open room with a well-stocked bar running the length of the room and a dark green and gold terrazzo floor.

Pak stood behind the bar greeting the officers, "Lt. Reeves, can I get you something to drink?" He said in perfect English.

Reeves ordered his usual, whiskey and water.

"It's going to turn as cold as a witch's tit here soon," said Sunderland, a warrant officer from Service Battery. "We're busy winterizing," he said by way of introduction to Caanen. Sunderland was in his early forties but appeared older and dissipated.

Officers from the three line batteries, A, B and C, as well as Headquarters and Service batteries trickled in to the club. It was mandatory for all officers to eat in the club every evening. This reduced fraternization with the non-commissioned soldiers, especially in the more remote line batteries. There were three large circular dinner tables, Lieutenant Colonel Fitzpatrick headed one table and Captain Dobbins was the senior officer at another. The third table was occupied by latecomers.

"Kitchen" Park stood near the swinging kitchen door,

"Tonight, we got beef with mushroom or meat wooaf," he shouted.

"I'll take the beef, Park," said Colonel Fitzpatrick, a short, muscular man with a youthful looking flat top. His morals were said to be straight from the Old Testament. He was as tidy and fastidious as the I Corps Commander above him and one of the fastest rising officers in the Army; he would make full colonel before he was forty.

"How do you like it so far Lt. Caanen?"

"I think it's beautiful, Sir," said Caanen, "particularly the mountainous area we're in."

Fitzpatrick looked at Caanen quizzically. "Hmm...keep busy and the time will pass quickly."

Fitzpatrick talked about his daughters to those seated at the head table. "When I return to the States, both of them plan to be married and we are going to have quite a festive night," he said. "My oldest is going to be a director in the Smithsonian and my youngest is pledged to a young lawyer in one of Cleveland's largest firms." The Colonel passed around a small photograph of the two. They were not unlike him, fair-haired, fair-skinned, healthy, athletic looking young women with their arms around each other's waist.

Park served dinner and Pak came from behind the bar and served drinks. Most of the officers had two or three drinks with their meal.

"We'll be going to L'l Chicago the day after tomorrow for firing range training," said the Colonel. "I want everyone to have their guns in shape—no screw ups this time."

On the last training exercise only six of the twelve guns left their compounds. Their immobility was blamed on lack of replacement parts. "Everything's sent to Nam— there's nothing left for Korea." However, Colonel Fitzpatrick blamed the ineptitude of the men, many of whom were 'McNamara Specials.' It was a fact, the war in Vietnam was stretching the Army very thin.

Caanen returned to his quarters around nine o'clock. Ahead of him he watched Reeves struggle with the handrail, weaving his way toward his hooch. Caanen searched through his collection of Dickens novels, each bound in black leather with gold tracing. He pulled down *Pickwick Papers*, and began to read.

THE "GOOKS"

It was bitterly cold the following morning and the men were in parkas and gloves. The hills surrounding Camp McIntyre stretched all the way to the Imjin River. The land was denuded of trees. Even small twigs were cut for kindling by old men who combed the steep hillsides each day. They made their way slowly downhill in the afternoon with A-frames on their backs overflowing with sticks and branches. These old 'Papa sans' dressed in traditional white smocks with the trousers fastened tightly at the ankle. Their heads were adorned with top hats or "khats" made of horsehair.

Smoke trailed slowly up into the clear sky in small puffs from the clay exhaust pipes that angled outward from the side of the village houses. A small stream that eventually made its way to the Imjin River was filled with sparkling water threading its way through the granite slag along the perimeter of the compound.

Clark, the company clerk, drove Caanen around to see the other batteries: A Battery was a short walk from Headquarters; B Battery was about two miles away from HQ and it was a full 5 mile drive to the entrance of C Battery hidden away in a small mountain chain. Caanen looked out of the jeep at the roadside rice paddies. Small children on wooden skates stumbled across the frozen paddies. The farmers were out in force dumping manure on the frozen paddies. Cattle pulled wooden wagons loaded with large ceramic jars laden with human waste. The honeycomb pattern of the rice paddies was broken only infrequently by a farmer's house. Most of the farmers lived in villages in homes with thatched roofs in a skein of alleyways. Caanen noticed one lone house that stood out on a small hilltop surrounded by statuesque Korean pines. Golden colored clay formed the maidan which shone brightly in the morning light along with the large wooden entrance gate to the household. There was great bucolic beauty in this austere land.

Clark drove skillfully, dodging large rocks scattered in the roadway. Top speed was 25 mph on the coarsely graveled roads riddled with ruts and potholes. The jeep passed pedestrians on the roadway, mostly older men, "Papasans." Neither the soldiers nor old men acknowledged one another.

"The Gooks don't want anything to do with us—they just want us to keep the North Koreans out," offered Clark.

The two drove to Bravo and Charley Batteries and then back to Alpha Battery on a little used trail. The village of Pamcoghi lay before them nestled into the flank of a hill. They descended the hill and entered the valley. This was the nearest village to battalion HQ. Each morning villagers left their houses and spread out on the multitude of foot trails coursing through the rice paddies. Some owned thin and wiry horses that now had their heavy winter coat. Small children accompanied the women. The cold wind made the two soldiers happy that the jeep was under canvas with a strong heater.

Clark brought the jeep to a halt at an intersection. One of the enduring memories of Korea was the hygiene of the rural folk. To the right were small hooch's aligned side by side and built over the streambed on a concrete apron. The concrete surface projected several feet beyond the buildings and ten feet above the river. Caanen saw three children on the apron squatting and relieving themselves with their winter leggings wrapped around their ankles. There was also an adult woman doing the same. The entire apron had visible collections of feces scattered over its surface for as far as one could see.

"WE'RE NOT GOING TO KILL ANYBODY!"

The following day the battalion was on the march by 0700 hours. Even in the cold the large tracked 8-inch guns created clouds of dust mixed with diesel fumes, which were intoxicating, announcing that the Battalion was on the move. The Battalion snaked its way northward to the firing range near the DMZ. The heavy guns caused the walls of the houses to tremble as they passed through the villages. Caanen came to like this part of soldiering very much. The sun rose above the mountains in front of him. He saw old men starting out from their homes to scour the hillsides for fuel. The grey granite cliffs added an aura of austerity and primitiveness to the scene. The cold penetrated the thin canvas lining of the jeep and the metal floorboard transferred the icy cold directly to his boot soles.

This idyllic mood was suddenly broken by the rasping, shushing sound of the PRC 6, the mobile phone. "Pull off the road until I arrive," shouted the Colonel over the radio.

Clark pulled the jeep over after passing through a small ville. A jeep was heading toward them at a rapid clip, dust swirling out behind it. The Colonel's jeep pulled up alongside them. Caanen walked over to the vehicle and saluted. Fitzpatrick tossed the speaker of the PRC 6 into the back of his jeep and stepped out.

"Damn it! Don't go any further up this road. There's been a catastrophe involving Bravo Battery."

The Colonel then filled him in on what had happened. Bravo Battery was making its way through a ville several miles up the road. The gun crews noticed as they entered the ville that the road was lined with Slicky Boys. The first three guns and their accompanying 10-ton ammo trucks passed through without incident. As the fourth gun entered the ville a Slicky Boy attempted to leap from the embankment onto the gun. He missed and fell under the tracks. He was dead by the time the gun stopped a few meters beyond. The body was crushed into the muddy soil and his face grotesquely contorted. The remaining Slicky Boys yelled at the gun crew and gestured angrily for several minutes and then fled when the local police arrived.

"I'm going to hear about this from I Corps," said the Colonel. This was Cannen's initiation into the violence in this cold Asian country, something that underlay its stark beauty.

Caanen later streaked forward in his jeep to the Headquarters Battery campsite. He arrived as darkness descended. Vehicles were scattered about with camouflage netting stretched over them. Some men had cut living vegetation and woven it into the netting. The communication section stood in stark contrast to the others. The crew had made no effort to camouflage their vehicles. The communications sergeant was one month from the end of his tour in Korea and often cut corners.

"All that netting will screw up our airwaves, Lieutenant," said Sgt. Stringer brashly. Caanen did not pursue the issue even though it was clearly against orders. What can you do with a short timer in Korea?

Several KATUSA (Korean Augmentation to United States Army) soldiers were stretching concertina wire around the periphery of the battery encampment.

"That shit isn't gonna hold the Slicky Boys," Reeves said. "You wait! Tonight, this place is going to be crawlin' with Slicky Boys and Mama Sans—they'll be in here all right. Nothing 'll stop 'em. I'm gonna walk around for a while," Reeves said as he descended into a deep arroyo outside the concertina wire. Mama Sans were walking up the gully carrying cloth bound foodstuff and trinkets on their heads.

"Alright, see ya later," said Caanen.

Later the mess sergeant served up a hot meal. The first sergeant made the list of the night watches and the men retired to their tents. Caanen slid into his sleeping bag and read Dickens with a flashlight.

Several hours later he shot bolt upright on his cot. "Reeves, get up! Someone's in the tent!"

A young man in black trousers and a white shirt was crawling on his belly while pulling Reeves's duffle bag. The lantern at the apex of the tent cast a faint beam of light on the ground. Caanen could see the man grimacing as he tugged at the bag. He slithered towards the edge of the tent.

Reeves brandished his pistol and pointed it at the young man. The Slicky Boy immediately released the bag and escaped under the tent flap.

"We'll check our losses in the morning," said Reeves climbing back into his sleeping bag after strapping his recovered duffle bag to his cot. Both he and Caanen slept with their pistols under their pillows.

The following morning Reeves met with section sergeants to discuss the breach of the company perimeter. A light dusting of snow had fallen during the early morning hours. The temperature was in the teens.

"No one was asleep, Sir. There was a massive infiltration and it was dark last night, no moon at all."

The communications sergeant burst into the conversation, "There's gonna be none of this shit again. We've Top Secret documents in our truck and no God damn Gook is going to get near them. Not while I'm here," he said patting the handle of his .45 caliber pistol. It was hard to know whether Sgt. Stringer was such a stickler for the rules or just wanted to engage in some dustup before going stateside. To "feel his oats", so to speak.

"Sergeant, I don't want anyone getting through the concertina tonight, but we're not going to kill anyone over it either," said Reeves.

Caanen left the group of men and started to make morning rounds around the campground. Someone had constructed a tent-like canopy with blankets around the back of a 3/4 ton truck including the exhaust pipe. The truck was idling. He wrenched the blankets away from the truck uncovering a KATUSA soldier lying on his left side, immobile. He was unarousable. Caanen pushed at his shoulders, moved his head and slapped his cheeks. There was no response. He began to compress the soldier's chest. Slowly the soldier's eyes opened and he suddenly lurched to his feet and began to dance around extravagantly, flailing his arms and legs.

Caanen yelled, "You all know better than this!" He looked around, all the soldiers had disappeared, fearing punishment for their part in abetting the man. "Sergeant Kim, take this man to the medics!"

Kim came on the double, looked at the soldier jerking about and guessed what had happened. Every line soldier had been warned about carbon monoxide poisoning and the prohibition of warming oneself with vehicle exhaust.

"I don't know if he's going to have any long range effects of the poisoning," Caanen said to Reeves.

"Oh, who gives a shit… One less Gook or two!" said Reeves matter of factly. Caanen was taken aback by Reeves's response and gave him a disapproving look. Reeves was unfazed. "Don't give me that shit! You haven't been here long enough. Tell me about it in 6 months, Lieutenant."

⁜

Later that day with the sun on the horizon, the encampment was lit with a golden glow from behind a mountain range hundreds of miles to the west. An hour later, in total darkness, HQ Battery began to turn in. The cold descended.

Caanen suddenly lurched awake, this time to the repeated firing of a pistol. There were shouts of, "Stop! Halt!"

Reeves and Caanen lifted the flap of the tent and walked toward the shouting in their long johns, pistols and flashlights in hand.

"What's all this about, Sgt. Stringer?" said Reeves.

"Some God damn Gook got in our truck and stole a radio with an encryption device. By God, he's a goner now."

"Shit!" said Reeves.

There were several more shots fired by perimeter guards.

"God damnit, stop that firing. Shit! Shit!" Reeves spat out.

The camp returned to darkness and quiet. There were no further disturbances that night.

The next morning Caanen started out early to inspect the campsite. He was lacing up his boots when Reeves returned from the latrine and grabbed him by the arm. He was bending over double.

"God damn it, Caanen, it hurts like hell when I piss. I've got the clap." "How could that be?"

"Oh, don't be such an ass. Whores were all over the place the other night, that's why I went on a walk."

Reeves sat in his jeep cupping his crotch while his driver drove him to Camp Red Cloud to see a medical officer.

Shortly after Reeves left there was a ruckus at the perimeter of the battery near the concertina wire. Men were shouting, Caanen ran towards the group of men huddled around an idling 3/4 ton truck.

"What's going on," shouted Caanen.

"Sir, Brown won't come to. We've dragged him out from out under the truck," said one of the men. The obtunded private had spread a canvas around the side of the truck and crawled underneath and fallen asleep and now was overcome with carbon monoxide poisoning. Suddenly the man began to thrash his head left and right, arose and began to walk.

"One of these days someone is going to be killed. I don't care how cold it gets outside, don't do what this fool did," shouted one of the sergeants.

Sgt. Stringer came charging up to Caanen carrying the missing encryption device. "Typical! Typical! The bastard! Once he realized he'd stolen Top Secret stuff he dumped it."

⁂

The battalion was to fire the guns in the morning and Caanen served as forward observer. He drove alone to the observer site. The last several miles were extremely rough with only two wheel tracks visible in the overgrown vegetation. He parked the jeep and threaded his way along a rarely used trail, stopping at the crest of a ridge. He looked over an enormous valley with a vast plain between converging mountain ranges. In the distance was a clump of trees near the confluence of two streams. The plain was covered with waist-high, feathery dried grasses that swayed gently back and forth in the breeze. He hollowed out a site to sit upon on the crest of the hill that allowed him to look over the entire terrain. He leaned against a small pine tree with his binoculars at his side. He called the fire center command on the PRC6 radio.

"Fire one round at coordinates…" Caanen and the fire center went back and forth on the radio, slowly marching the explosions closer to the clump of trees. Following each explosion, he corrected the range and deflection.

"Left 100 and Add 200, over."

Caanen heard someone approaching through the shrubbery over his left shoulder.

"Caanen, my God! Fancy finding you here," shouted Frank Pacinni.

"What ill wind brings you up here Pacinni?"

"I'm forward observer for a 175 unit. Jesus! I'm freezing already and I just got out of the jeep."

Pacinni spread a sleeping bag on the ground over some pine needles. He got into the bag with all his winter clothing including his boots. He raised his head, leaned forward and brought the binoculars to his eyes.

"Doesn't look like you went too far in this man's Army, does it Caanen?" "No, not yet. You're the last person I would expect to show up over here."

Caanen knew Pacinni thought he was a fool for taking the Army seriously and attempting to succeed as an officer.

Pacinni scooted forward for comfort in the sleeping bag. "They wanted to send me to Nam, but the orders were cancelled at the last minute. My foot never did heal. I think they were frustrated and sent me over here."

"How's your foot now?"

"Couldn't be better."

Pacinni reached for the radio, "One round at coordinates...?" Caanen glanced at his map and gestured toward Pacinni,

"You've misread the coordinates Pacinni—what you called in is directly in front of us a thousand yards or so. Call them back and stop the round."

"Relax, Caanen. It'll be alright," said Pacinni as he put his head back on the sleeping bag and stared into the steel grey welkin.

A minute later both officers could hear a whistling sound close above their heads, perhaps less than a hundred yards away followed by a ground shaking explosion. The round struck at the base of the hill they were sitting on. Pacinni saw dust rising just above his feet. He twisted in the sleeping bag, sat up and stared at the flying debris.

"Jesus Christ! Add 6000 and fire again," he shouted into the radio handset. Caanen informed his fire center that he was terminating the exercise for the day. "I'm not staying up here with you and get my ass blown off—not for someone groveling around in a sleeping bag." The 175 mm howitzer was a notoriously inaccurate artillery piece and Caanen had little confidence in Pacinni's ability to read a map or call in fire.

Pacinni raised his head again and munched on a candy bar.

"Gotta keep warm," he said, "You know, you always took the Army a little too seriously, Caanen."

Caanen drove back to HQ encampment. The following morning the entire battalion made its way back to Camp McIntyre without incident.

"GENTLEMEN, GRAB YOUR DRINKS"

E very new officer underwent initiation in the Officers Club. Colonel Fitzpatrick was not fond of these events, but he didn't moderate the ferocity with which his junior officers planned for the initiates—the new officers would be toasted with alcohol until they fell over.

Cpt. Dobbins took charge of the initiation while standing at the bar. Dobbins was a large man still in his twenties, but looked older, a former lineman for the University of Missouri football team and an ROTC graduate. His abdomen hung over his waistline.

Everyone was intimidated by his great size. Pak placed two small Kim chi jars on the bar.

Dobbins read a paragraph about the symbolism of the shield and crest of the 1st of the 17th. "The field of the shield is red, the artillery color. The principal charge is the castle of Ehrenbreitstein bedruised by a bendlet carrying the American colors and seventeen stars, to signify the occupation of the castle by the 17th Field Artillery..."

Pak was busy pouring alcoholic beverages into the Kim chi jars: a dash of this, a dash of that, some crème de menthe, some Chevez Regal...

Dobbins droned on, "Our motto is: In Time of Peace Prepare for War!"

Pak stirred the poisonous mixture and handed the Kim chi jars to Dobbins who passed them on to Caanen and Lt. Schuette.

"Gentlemen grab your drinks. Let's welcome these two officers to Korea! Drink up!"

At his command all the other officers raised their glasses and sipped. Schuette and Caanen were admonished to drink fast and long. Schuette tried to enjoy the concoction. Caanen was alarmed and protested that he did not drink alcohol. The colonel smiled and continued to sip his drink. Thirty minutes later Schuette and Caanen struggled to their hooch, falling on the trail, losing their dress hats and Caanen vomited on the paving stones. There was no reading Dickens that night.

⁂

Headquarters Battery First Sgt. Williams informed Caanen the following morning that Lt. Reeves had left for the medical clinic at Red Cloud once again. He smiled knowingly. Although Williams was only in his early forties he was coarsened by alcohol and tobacco. He chain-smoked Camels and had a hacking, productive cough. His closest companion was a squat dog, known as Frog, whose hind limbs were strikingly shorter than his fore limbs. His hair was tinged green at the shoulders and dark burgundy spots covered his hindquarters. Frog was habituated to alcohol and was very bad tempered when it was withheld from him. Caanen was not fond of Williams or Frog, but he feared Frog more since he often lurked near sidewalks growling at pedestrians.

In evenings after work the non-coms walked to their club with Frog at their flank. He had a special place at the bar next to Sgt. Williams who poured beer and whiskey into his dish. Frog lapped up the libations.

Caanen occasionally encountered Frog on his nightly walk to the theatre where he was assigned as movie officer for the battalion and his presence was required almost every night. The 35-mm projector needed frequent repairs and there was no heating in the theatre. A handful of men with their parka hoods pulled over their heads to keep warm were scattered amongst the many seats. Occasionally the theatre was closed for months awaiting parts for the projector, but it had been running nightly for several weeks.

After locking up the theatre one evening Caanen started back to his hooch. He was passing the non-com club. The entrance to the club was five feet above the sidewalk leading up to it and the door of the club was open, casting light onto Caanen's path. Suddenly there was a shadow. Caanen glanced just in time to duck the lunging Frog with his mouth agape. The dog crumpled into a heap six feet beyond Caanen who backed away slowly as Frog shook himself back to consciousness.

The following morning Caanen brought up the incident with First Sgt. Williams.

"That animal should be put down. It's dangerous," said Caanen.

"You don't understand, Sir, "Williams said unctuously, "Frog has had a rough life, not the least part of which was dodging all the Gooks who wanted to eat him. I don't think he'll do that again— I'll see to it." Although dogs were a delicacy for many Koreans, preserving Frog from that fate only left him to terrorize the men.

At dinner that evening Colonel Fitzpatrick informed Caanen that he would represent the Battalion at Camp Stanley the following day at a rally and speech by President Johnson. Johnson was the first US President to ever visit Korea; he was warmly received by the South Koreans and it was said he was enjoying his trip.

Caanen arrived at Camp Stanley in the late afternoon. The sky was uniformly grey and bitingly cold. A large outdoor amphitheater was filled with troops and large speakers were hoisted on poles around the perimeter so that everyone could hear the address. The audience was in woolen khakis and there was much stomping of feet and clapping of hands to keep warm as they waited for the President. After arriving Johnson praised the sacrifices made by the soldiers. He also praised the efforts of South Korea, which had recently sent troops to Vietnam. In the excitement of talking to the troops he fibbed a little, claiming that one of his ancestors had died at the Alamo. The President stayed overnight at Walker Hill Resort in Seoul. The following article appeared in the New York *Times*:

> *"While President Johnson slept in a resort in Seoul, North Koreans attacked an outpost on the DMZ killing six US soldiers and one KATUSA in "hand-to-hand combat."*
> **New York Times, November 3, 1966**

Kim Il Sung was pursuing his 'foreign policy' although little notice was taken of it back in the States. His policy consisted of only unconventional warfare directed against both US and ROK troops in an attempt to weaken the diplomatic and military bond between the two countries.

Caanen left for HQ. Battery after Johnson's speech. Although he arose each day moved by its austere beauty of the land, there was also the excitement of being a line officer in the US Army with the enemy only miles away. When North Korean troops were on an exercise a great cloud of dust would rise into the atmosphere to the North.

"GOD DAMN IT, WHY DON'T YOU PLAY RIGHT?"

Colonel Fitzpatrick was assigned stateside. A week after his departure the new Battalion Commander arrived. Lt. Colonel Carrick was not a 'golden boy.' For one thing, he looked older than Fitzpatrick. His family was stateside in Fort Leavenworth, Kansas. The unhappiness in his voice was palpable on his recounting of his leave from his wife and daughter. This was his first stint in Korea. He would rather have been assigned to Vietnam where he could have at least advanced his career. He was lean, wore a doleful expression and was uncongenial. Major Wilson introduced him to the other officers at dinner. The Colonel refused to undergo the initiation ceremony much to the dismay of Dobbins.

"I don't get it! Everyone's initiated, why not him. Something ain't right," Dobbins said.

"After my initiation and being so sick the next day, I guess I agree with you," said Schuette.

Several officers played ping-pong in the adjoining recreation room. Lt. Wurtz, the Battery Commander of Bravo Battery, put so much spin on the ball it was impossible to hit anything but the net on return of his serve. Caanen felt frustrated hitting the net nine out of ten times. He began to harbor a growing dislike of Wurtz: it just seemed a little rum the way he always won even though his serve was agonizingly slow. Lt. Samuels thought he would make a stab at playing Wurtz. This was the long and short of the battalion officers' corps: Wurtz, 5'6" tall, red headed, and self-assured and Samuels, 6'4", gangly, black and the butt of his own jokes. Wurtz began with his left-handed spinning serves and it soon exasperated Samuels. Samuels began swearing.

"God damn it, Wurtz! Why don't you play right?"

Colonel Carrick presided at the head table at dinner that night. After dinner was served, the junior officers returned to their former pastimes, drinking and playing Ping-Pong. Carrick returned to the bar to drink. Several hours later Caanen observed him walking rigidly to his hut.

∞

December was bitterly cold. The guards at the main gate could not be coaxed out of the guardhouse. They huddled around a space heater in the small, poorly insulated shed. One guard became the focus of a major battalion hullabaloo. Private Butts was forty years old, divorced and friendless. He had joined the Army on three separate occasions having nothing better to do. He stood in morning formation disheveled and unshaven. Sgt. Williams became angrier and angrier at morning head count, there being no improvement in Butt's dress. Finally, Williams had it with Pvt. Butts, what with his pant cuffs not tucked into his boots, his dirty blouses and unbuttoned jackets.

"God damn it, Butts. That's it. You're on the night shift, main gate guard duty for a month!"

Butts responded with, "Right Sarge. Wilco" and a silly grin.

Reeves wanted Caanen to follow up on Butts to ensure he was actually awake during his night shifts. Caanen arose late one evening in order to check on Butts. He could hear the wind howling outside his hooch. The air inside was already frigid in spite of two glowing space heaters. Caanen stepped outside. Heavy snow was falling inside the lighted arc of the perimeter lights. He saw one civilian guard walking alongside the concertina wire almost obscured by driving snow.

Caanen carefully made his way downhill to the main gate guardhouse. The weak incandescent bulb was visible through the window. No one was standing inside the guardhouse. Caanen looked around. Maybe Butts was walking outside to keep awake or smoking. Caanen waited for several minutes. He then let himself into the guardhouse to phone the main switchboard. Butts was stretched out on the floor asleep, his rifle beside him, next to the space heater. Caanen shouted,

"Get up Private Butts! Now!"

Butts turned to his right side and brought his hand up to shield his eyes. Caanen knelt over the soldier. He reeked of alcohol.

The following morning Lt. Reeves had Butts at attention before his desk when Caanen entered.

"You could have had us all murdered in the middle of the night. I'm taking half your paycheck for this, you sorry bastard! Now get out of here."

Butts was to personally fail Lt. Reeves once again, several months later.

Even though few in the military at the time had seen active duty during the Korean War 14 years before—that was another generation of soldier--the legend of brutal warriors was still current among the older soldiers who had served before in this frozen land. The kitchen help and houseboys often spoke of the Turks and what formidable soldiers they were with their swift, decisive justice. It was said that petty crime had become rampant since the last compound of Turkish soldiers packed it in and left for home.

One day Clark and Caanen were driving with MSgt Williams sitting in the back seat when he suddenly yelled, "Stop!" Clark pulled the jeep off the gravel road.

"Off to the right, over there," Williams said, pointing. "See the concrete steps over there? That was the entrance to the last Turkish compound in Korea. The last stint I had here, soldiers were still here. They had one row of concertina wire surrounding the entire compound, that's all. You entered through the gate at the steps. There were a dozen Quonset huts scattered around and maybe 150 soldiers. They had hundreds of Koreans working on the compound and there was never even a theft of so much as a pair of socks. As my houseboy says, 'No one fuck around in Turk compound—cut nuts off.' And it was true, one time I came by this way and two Korean workers were hanging from each gatepost—they had been caught stealing wool blankets."

Clark threw the jeep into gear. Williams said, "I remember that they had big knives strapped to their waists. That's how they punished crooks; cutting off fingers— they were a scary group." All three men marveled at the prospect of such swift justice especially since their days were filled with complaints of petty theft. Every movement of the Army through Korean villages invited the ubiquitous Slicky Boys, the most gifted of thieves.

After returning to HQ Compound a Staff Sergeant approached Caanen late in the afternoon as the men were dispersing to their barracks.

"Sir! Would you like to join our battery basketball team? Can you play?" he asked.

"Yes, alright, I'll help you out."

"Be at the gym around 1700 hours."

The gymnasium was located in the Service Battery area. Caanen arrived early and warmed up. He was slow and a poor dribbler, but an accurate shooter.

That evening Headquarters Battery played Alpha Battery. Caanen was joined by six other players from HQ. He was the tallest on the HQ team at 6'2". As they huddled together Caanen glanced at the opposition. He now realized he was the only officer on the court. Staff Sgt. Davis of Alpha Battery was a really big man, 250 pounds and four inches taller than Caanen. Alpha Battery also had athletic smaller men who could dribble and shoot.

The A Battery guard brought the ball down the court and passed to Davis who immediately wheeled toward the basket and struck Caanen across the nose with his left forearm. Caanen staggered off the court. A Battery was soon up by 20 points and Davis was unstoppable. Caanen went back into the game, took a pass and moved toward the basket for a layup. Davis crashed into him sending him spinning toward the sidelines.

"Sorry Sir," said Davis, his teeth shining and sweat dripping off of his black torso—A Battery was skins.

Caanen hobbled to his team's huddle at halftime.

"Don't worry about it, Sir. You're the only officer and they're going to take it out on you," said one of Caanen's teammates.

Thirty minutes later Caanen was walking haltingly to his hooch. He got off only one shot and missed. He thought he had torn a groin muscle. Davis came up to him, grinned, and said,

"See you again, Sir."

DOCTOR ZHIVAGO

The Battalion theatre was closed for over a month while awaiting replacement parts for the 35-mm projector. Caanen gave every soldier a pass to attend a showing of *Doctor Zhivago* in a nearby infantry fort where the theatre was functioning.

Caanen and Clark also decided to attend the movie. Clark drove past Bravo Battery and turned up a sharply inclined hill, past a ville and began to descend slowly toward the infantry fort. The ground was frozen and old snow lay along the roadside. A light powdery snow was falling, but the sun was out at the same time and warming the air.

"Wait a minute! Stop, Clark! That looks like a person there on the side of the road," said Caanen. Lying in a clump of snow that had been graded off the road was a sack-like object covered by a parka. Caanen got out of the jeep and approached the lump. It was a man. He rolled him onto his back and shouted at him,

"Hey! Get up!"

He was a rough looking Korean man in his forties. He smelled of fermented maekju. He had not shaved for days. The skin on one side of his face was blotched with red and purple. The man could not be aroused.

"This guy's going to freeze out here. Can we take him to a nearby hospital?" "They won't let us take him into the fort, Sir. There isn't any nearby civilian hospital. He'll be okay, you see this stuff all the time," said Clark leaning on the steering wheel of the jeep.

The man groaned and rolled back onto to his abdomen. "Ken cha..naaah…("no sweat")," he moaned.

Caanen had a difficult time enjoying *Doctor Zhivago*. His thoughts kept returning to the drunk on the roadside that day. Here was a country where one looked after oneself, rarely one's neighbor.

When Clark and Caanen drove back to battalion, the man was no longer to be seen. The episode troubled Canaan for months. He ruminated over what had become of the man and he felt that he should have done more in spite of the rules.

～∞～

Caanen was jubilant upon learning from Major Wilson that Lt. Lehrer was to join the battalion as Service Battery Commander. His initiation at the Officers' Club went off without a hitch. Lehrer easily consumed Pak's toxic concoction of alcohol without ill effects.

Service Battery was in need of some fresh blood and Lehrer was eager to address the part shortages for the vehicles and get the guns back online. He relied heavily on the experience of Warrant Officer Sunderland. Sunderland ordered the appropriate parts and organized the mechanics' workload to get the machinery operational. His knowledge of self-propelled guns was greater than anyone in the battalion. Caanen went to him about vehicle issues in HQ battery. Caanen, Sunderland and Lehrer formed a loose brotherhood at the Officers Club. The latter two enjoyed their whiskey and water and stayed late at the club each night. Caanen went early to his hooch to meet a KATUSA corporal who came several times a week to instruct him in the orthography and pronunciation of Korean. The instruction began with a paperback grade school primer.

One evening after serving dinner at the Officers' Club, Kitchen Park invited Caanen to his home in Kumgongni, a ville close to B Battery. This was a forbidden destination for officers. Caanen arrived a little after noon dressed in fatigues. He waited in a bar on the main street that had recently turned to soft mud and ice. Several barmaids spoke to him as he stood inside the sliding rice paper covered door escaping a gentle rain.

"You want'ee drink, Ru-tenent?"

"No, thank you, I don't."

"Oh, come on, Ru-tenent."

Park opened the sliding door. "Hi Ru-tenent. Follow me." His breath smelled heavily of fermented drink. "Maekju," said Park miming drinking from a bottle. One of the chief characteristics of Park was his fluency in languages. Although he spoke English with the usual accentuation of Koreans, he was intelligent and knowledgeable in the ways of the military. His view of Americans was coarsened by the years of rubbing elbows with lonely and homesick young men.

The two wound their way along slippery, muddy walking trails between small huts and larger houses, keeping under the eaves to avoid the rain. Fog was settling in and there was a yellowish halo around the incandescent bulbs fastened near entrance doors. Caanen could hear the monotonous and deep drumming of the city's 2-cycle diesel generator. It was soothing after a while, like waves on a beach. The two men reached Park's house, removed their footwear and stepped onto the wooden floor of the rectangular room. Blankets and furniture were stacked against one of the walls on the wooden floor. There was a chest of drawers, but no chairs. Another door at the end of the room led directly to the kitchen. The floor of the kitchen was rammed earth. Park introduced his wife who bowed from her waist to Caanen. She was neatly dressed and younger than Park. Caanen looked into the kitchen at the various bowls and wooden cooking implements laid out on a low table.

The fireplace was in the kitchen. Soft anthracite coal was molded into cylinders about ten inches in diameter, and ten inches in height and drilled through lengthwise with ½-inch channels allowing for airflow and an even burning of the entire cylinder of coal. These cylinders were placed with tongs on top of the previously burned cylinder. The heated air flowed beneath the floor of the living space through a conduit and the smoke exited on the opposite side of the hooch through a clay pipe chimney that barely cleared the eaves. Carbon monoxide generated by the slowly burning coal could reach lethal levels in houses especially when the outside air was still. When this occurred, there was little air movement in the rooms.

Park and Caanen sat down in the living room and Park's wife served maekju, a coarse rice beer. Park assured Caanen he would eventually acquire a taste for the malty liquid. The drink had the unmistakable aroma of fermented rice.

The topic of conversation changed to the defense of Korea.

"Realry, Ko-reans not worry about North. If they attack, we die. The DMZ is own-ry miles that way," Park said gesturing with his arm toward the north.

"Don't you think it is worth fighting to keep your country?"

"Ko-reans no care. We live day to day. It will be same if they come or not. We say, ken-channa. It mean, no sweat," he put out his cigarette in the ashtray.

The men sat cross-legged while Park's wife served rice and fiery hot Kim chi. She had lustrous black hair bobbed short in the back. She wore startlingly red lipstick and rouge on her cheeks and walked with a soft shuffle on the wooden floor. Caanen was enchanted.

The drinking increased, in part to quench the burning peppery aftertaste of the Kim chi. The men pulled out the bedrolls and lay down for a nap. Several hours later Caanen arose, awakened by the warm blankets beneath him heated from the floor. The rain had turned to snow. He started back to HQ. The light snowfall covered the bill of his ball cap. Smoke was slowly curling up into the air from the scattered farmhouse chimneys. The northern skies were dark. It was likely there would be 6 inches of snow or more by morning. On his walk back to the battery Canaan noted the deep silence surrounding him and the stark beauty of the mountain scape. He was giddy with a sense of expansiveness and appreciation of the beauty of this stark land.

A FIASCO

The Colonel informed every officer at dinner that a field exercise was forthcoming. He expected perfect execution. Samuels and Jacobs carried on in *sotto voce* beneath the colonel's monotone. They had their own brand of humor at the far table.

"It's January for God's sake, why don't we cancel this until spring?" Jacobs said in a hushed voice.

"I'm from Georgia, not Greenland for Christ's sake," said Samuels. "Besides, my black ass is gonna' get frostbitten."

The exercise was going to be difficult to perform since four of the twelve battalion 8-inch artillery pieces were not operable, due to the lack of spare parts. No one was anxious to man the iron monsters anyway. The gun crews were forced to stand on the cold pieces for hours during firing and had no protection from the wind. Even in winter clothing, the soldiers were cold. An ungloved hand stuck to the cold iron machine ended invariably with skin being torn off when the hand was removed.

The battalion started movement at 0700 hours. Four hours later Canaan was in the advance party reconnoitering a site for HQ Battery.

"We'll site the encampment here, Sgt. Williams," said Canaan. An hour later he was in the Battalion G3 2½ ton van with Colonel Carrick listening to the radio traffic as the field batteries maneuvered into place. Jacobs and Samuels were leading A and B batteries, respectively, to their locations.

"This is Alpha 2, I'm at a dead end out here. I can't figure it out. Goddamn it, over!"

"This is Bravo 2. I'm totally lost out here. There is no place to put the guns. It's all a big ravine, over!"

Colonel Carrick suddenly broke into the chatter, "Calling Alpha 2 and Bravo 2, over."

"This is Bravo 2 sir, over,"

"**Not SIR!** You've compromised the code you Simpleton, **OUT!**" Samuels responded with, "**Sorry, Sir.**"

A handful of I Corps officers were observing the battalion exercise, one of whom overheard the exchange on the radio. Canaan saw him entering his observations in a spiral notebook. A half hour later Colonel Carrick was still fuming.

"Are we ready to site in those guns, Lieutenant?"

"No sir. Neither Alpha nor Bravo battery are in place."

"Shit! Samuels and Jacobs are idiots! I'm tempted to relieve them of their duties." "I could go out there and reconnoiter. I think I know where Jacobs might be." "Do it, or we'll never get these guns registered for firing today."

Canaan drove out in the general direction of Alpha battery. The jeep driver pulled up to the crest of a hill.

"There they are. Let's go over there. Jacobs just led everyone up a blind alley." "Yes, Sir. Hard to imagine how he did that," Clark said, smirking.

Canaan got out of the jeep and talked to Jacobs who was gesturing to everyone to back up their vehicle. This included 23 vehicles stretched out in a line a mile long.

"Shit! What a mess. The Colonel's gonna have my ass over this," Jacobs shouted in between gesturing to the drivers.

"What possessed you to drive up this road. You can see it can't possibly pass over the next hill. You just needed to go straight a little further."

"I've never driven anywhere before now, Caanen. Really! I grew up in Manhattan, taking buses and subways—never drove. Goddamn it!" Finally, Jacobs got the unit straightened out.

Samuels extricated his battery from a ravine and led them to the proper spot. Because of the confusion and lost time the drivers were in a rush. One KATUSA soldier was thrown from the back of a ¼ ton truck onto his head. He lay on the roadway unconscious. He was later air evacuated by helicopter with a concussion and head injury. This cast a pall over the remainder of the exercise. The mission was deadly earnest and there was no easy way to soften the violent happenings that were a function of the tasks and the machines employed. 'Not a death like the last outing but violence none the less,' thought Caanen, reflecting on the day's happenings.

⚜

"We're going back into the field again and do this thing right," said Colonel Carrick. "I've never seen such an unprepared group of officers and soldiers. It was Keystone Cops out there."

Three weeks after the last training debacle the battalion was headed back to the field. Korea was locked in snow and ice.

Clark drove Caanen to the destination he was to determine where to site HQ battery. The jeep crested a precipice on the graveled road heading to Lil' Chicago and onto a bridge; they could see the Imjin River curving gently as it came from the north and turned westward. The water was a dark green. Snow swirled about the jeep screen.

"My God, look down there, Sir," said Clark pointing to a formation of well over a hundred ROK soldiers standing on the bank of the river. Both men got out of the vehicle and peered at the sight directly below them. A ROK Captain in fatigues stood waist high in the freezing water and gestured to the others to wade out into the current. The men held their rifles above their heads and slowly waded out to mid-chest high depth of water. There was no noise save for the crackling of thin ice near the banks of the river and the surge of the current.

Caanen looked at Clark and gestured for them to get back in the jeep. "Jesus Christ, Sir, these gooks are tough sons-of-a-bitches. That is all I can say," said Clark.

Several miles further on Caanen supervised the fording of the Imjim by the line batteries. The ford was a quarter of a mile of surging water upstream of a rickety wooden bridge and over a man's head in depth. A line of heavy ammo trucks and 8" guns waited at the river's edge for a signal to cross. Caanen walked the wooden planks of the delicate bridge peering over at the clear, brownish water. Long wisps of algae formed a skirt around the concrete pylons. High water had scoured out a deep basin from beneath the bridge. Caanen waved the lead vehicle on and then walked slowly keeping pace with the 8-inch gun as it traversed the river. Occasionally the gun plunged forward dipping its barrel in the water. The driver was also submerged briefly when low points in the streambed were encountered. The heavy tracked vehicle kept plowing headlong, the powerful diesel engine sporadically muffled by waves that struck the front of the engine casing. The fording was successful and without incident.

The following day Cannen was the forward observer for this exercise and after siting HQ battery he drove out to a lonely outpost. He stood below a large pine tree to escape the wind and blowing snow that sheared across the mountaintop. The firing range was a large triangular area covered with a red dust pulverized by thousands of artillery rounds. The apex of the triangle faced towards him. A deep and turbulent river cut a gorge around the triangle. Caanen raised his binoculars and saw men, women and children busy within an enormous cave cut into the side of the river gorge. The firing range was not 'open' before 10 o'clock in the morning and many people were still scavenging the range for pieces of shells. There was a good local market for brass. Promptly at 0945 hours the scavengers began streaming towards the gorge, down over the cliff side and into the cave. They used a stolen shortwave radio to monitor the firing orders of the various units that used the firing range. Caanen swept the range with his glasses and finding no humans, called in the first round.

Four hours and countless rounds later, snow squalls began to appear in the valley, sometimes obscuring the firing range. Caanen halted firing, often for as long as thirty minutes. He watched the brass pickers, women and children racing up the side of the gorge and out onto the range whenever there was a lull in the firing. At one point there was a cessation of snowfall and an unobstructed view of the firing range. The brass pickers were in their cave. Caanen called for a round. Forty-five seconds later heavy snow began falling on the firing range. Caanen, sensing a potential problem called the fire center. It was too late. A round was on the way. Caanen caught glimpses of the gorge and cave and could see the brass pickers racing out from the cave and up onto the firing range as snow fell around them. They were confident firing had ceased. Five seconds later, Caanen could hear a muffled explosion in the distance. Snow was now engulfing the Forward Observer site as well.

Later that night Caanen was awakened from deep sleep. He made his way to the HQ van. Colonel Carrick looked glum. There were several full colonels from I Corps present.

"Lieutenant, did you observe any stray rounds today?"

"No Sir. I didn't."

"Three brass pickers were killed today on the range, a woman, man and nine year-old child. The chief of the brass pickers is certain that one of our rounds did it."

"You didn't call fire in the blind, did you?"

"No Sir. It's possible that our last round could have hit someone. They came streaming out of the cave because of heavy snowfall thinking we had stopped, but a round was on its way already."

"Well, I Corps is going to take down the details on this. You won't be doing any forward observing until this is cleared up."

Caanen returned to his tent with a deep sense of unease.

FROG AND AN EIGHTH ARMY EXERCISE

For months Caanen's sleep was disturbed by vivid dreams of the gorge. In the dream he stood alone on a precipice overlooking a surging river running through a cavernous abyss. Small children huddled below the edge of a cliff spread out in front of him. Then snow began to fall in a blinding curtain and simultaneously the children raced up a stone staircase. Caanen shouted to the children to stop. He awakened at this point frightened and cold.

Months later Caanen could no longer recall exactly what had happened on that freezing afternoon in the waning light. Did these deaths have any "meaning"? He concluded that they did not, they merely happened, like any other event that day.

In spite of Caanen's foreboding over the firing range investigation the mood in the officer's club days later was exhilaration. It had been a successful field exercise. Colonel Carrick wanted Caanen to go out the following morning and reconnoiter another firing range for a future field exercise.

Clark was driving. The canvas shell of the jeep was battened down for warmth.

Sgt. Williams sat in the back seat with Frog.

Williams said to Caanen, "He'll be good Sir. Don't worry."

Dirty snow lay at the roadside, melting during the day and freezing at night. Compacted ice covered the roadway. Clark put chains on the rear tires of the jeep. After an hour of driving they entered a valley dotted with steep hills. The firing range was somewhere in front of them. Caanen gestured to Clark to drive up a hill that had obviously been driven on before—tire tracks could be seen going up the side of the incline.

Clark started the jeep up the incline and drove three or four hundred yards. The vehicle was approaching the crest, which was now in sunlight. The ground was thawing into icy mud. Suddenly the tires and chains began spinning. The engine whined. Clark unthinkingly put the clutch in and pressed on the brakes. The vehicle stopped and then slowly started to slide backwards, picking up speed.

Williams was shouting from the back, "Let the clutch out. Keep going! God damn it, Clark!"

Instead of letting out the clutch, Clark reached for the hand brake and wrenched the steering wheel to the left. The vehicle turned slightly, paused and then rolled onto its side and began to tumble downhill. It came to rest on the passenger side. Clark was dangling from the driver's seat over Caanen and Williams was trying to remove Frog from underneath him. Frog was growling ominously. Clark was able to climb out of the jeep and right it.

Caanen, Williams and Frog jolted upright. Caanen stepped out of the vehicle followed by Williams and a trembling Frog. Caanen looked down the hill. They were still several hundred yards from the valley floor where they had started. Mud was caking their boots. Frog continued to growl menacingly.

"I don't know about this animal," said Caanen.

"He'll behave," said Williams. Caanen could smell alcohol. Clark nodded his head knowingly to Caanen and gestured with his hand toward William's hip pocket. Wet shards of glass were sticking through the fabric.

"Come on Frog. Get back in here. Com'on boy!" Williams climbed into the jeep after Frog. Clark started downhill in first gear.

The vehicle skidded on frozen mud as it descended to the valley floor. The odor of alcohol permeated the jeep.

◦◦◦

At dinner Colonel Carrick informed everyone that the Battalion would be participating in a Pacific Theatre exercise and Caanen would be detailed to G3, Eighth Army for the duration of the exercise.

Caanen drove south to Yongsan and Eighth Army HQ, now stationed in the field. He joined the G3 personnel who were loading equipment into a paneled room on a deuce and half truck truck bed. This would be his station for the next three days. The van was parked in a forested rear area. An armed guard stood outside the entrance 24 hours a day. Camouflage netting was stretched over the vehicles. The weather was dry and bitterly cold. The high for the day was 10 degrees Fahrenheit and was punctuated with brief bursts of blinding snowfall.

Caanen was to assist Colonel Savage, the G3, who greeted Caanen with a cigar stub in his mouth. He was short, squat and sported a one-day's growth of stubble on his chin. He had his helmet liner on with a small 'full bird' insignia stenciled on the front.

"Get that helmet on son. You gotta wear that anytime you're out of this van." The two men entered the van outfitted inside with two large situational maps on the walls, a bank of phones, and cryptographic devices in cabinets. There were two small hatches that opened outwards to allow fresh air to enter the room.

"I want you back here in an hour and we're gonna start populating these maps with the unit positions" Savage said removing his helmet and attempting to light his cigar stub.

Caanen went to find his cot in a nearby tent. An attaché from the ROK Army, 2nd Lt. Kim, shared the tent with Caanen. Kim was a graduate of Seoul University and spoke impeccable English. He was tall, thin and handsome with closely cropped hair groomed with a shiny hair oil. He continued unpacking his suitcase when Caanen arrived at the tent.

"Afternoon," said Caanen.

"I guess we will be getting to know one another," said Kim. "Maybe I can improve my English while I am here."

Kim had a degree in theology and was absorbed in the teachings of Karl Barth, particularly his sermons against the Nazis. Caanen, embarrassed, admitted he didn't know anything of the man but the name. Kim sat on his cot, opened a bound notebook and began writing.

"I'm still working on my thesis. I want to finish it and go to the University of Chicago for advanced studies. My work is on Barth and his influence on modern Protestantism." Caanen was surprised and impressed that this handsome man took religion so seriously. Every time Kim had a break in his duties he returned to the tent and wrote in his notebook.

Caanen returned to the van. He and Colonel Savage spent several hours locating and marking with a pin the exact coordinates of each of the Eighth Army units on the situation board. The phone board occasionally rang and Caanen answered the calls—they were from unit G3 officers registering their coordinates.

"You and I will be taking 24-hour call in this room. At least one of us needs to be here all the time. If something really big happens and you're here alone, send the guard to wake me up," said Savage.

Caanen relieved Colonel Savage that evening. Savage's fatigues were wrinkled and the stubble longer. He had been napping on a makeshift cot.

"The exercise is coming along. It looks as if the North may be trying a ground attack further east. You can see where I have moved half our units. You'll get new position reports all night," Savage said as he walked out of the van.

Twelve hours later Savage re-entered the van. He was clean-shaven and rested. Caanen saw that it was still dark outside. Savage asked for a status report. Caanen gave a detailed account of units and manpower and their deployment. He pointed out which ones had nuclear capabilities. Savage sent the data forward through the encryption device.

"Hit the sack, I'll see you later," Savage said.

Caanen's breath was visible as he walked slowly to the tent. Lt. Kim was in his bedroll. Caanen climbed into his sleeping bag after removing only his boots. Later in the afternoon when he arose and sat forward on his cot he found Kim writing intently in his notebook.

"I hope to publish my thesis as a book after I receive my degree," Kim said. His uniform even after a day of work was pressed and clean. His black hair had a neat part on the left side and shone with Vitalis.

"Are you married, Kim?"

"No, not enough time for that. My parents are upset about it though. They want me to marry a woman from a family that we have known for years."

Caanen left the tent to relieve Savage for the last time. Colonel Savage poured some whiskey from his canteen into his mess kit cup. He held out the cup to Caanen, "Want some son? Maybe you should make a career of the Army. You've a gift for organization. By the way that business regarding the deaths on the firing range is all cleared up. No problem." The following day all the units returned to their home bases. Caanen carried his duffle bag with its soiled winter clothing into his hooch. Living under tents is difficult at any time, but in intense, unremitting cold it was difficult not only to keep warm, but clean as well.

MONA

During the first winter in Korea Caanen came to know the local haberdashers quite well. Two Korean tailors occupied a Quonset hut not far from Caanen's hooch. He had rarely worn a suit previously and here were Park and Park offering to make any number of suits from fine fabrics for a pittance. Caanen felt effusive and in some complicated reasoning felt he was making for good relations between the Americans and Koreans by spending his money on civilian dress. As winter deepened in Chosun, Caanen hatched the idea of modifying the heavy and inelegant winter clothing for officers. He took the winter outer trousers to the tailor and had the legs tapered with a slit on the lateral aspect of the leg with large buttons to tighten the fabric around the calf.

As is probably true of many young men in their early twenties, Caanen sought some metaphysical explanation for his residing in the Republic of Korea. He kept a diary—entering short, sometimes muddle-headed concepts regarding metaphysics, psychology, psychoanalysis and sexuality on almost a nightly basis early in his assignment to Korea. Eventually he ceased entering anything in the thick handbook that he had purchased before going to the Yucatan.

The rumor in the officers' club was that the Colonel was going to shake up the line battery commanders because their performance was below standard. That evening the Colonel announced changes that would take place in several weeks. Lt. Reeves was to take over C Battery.

After dinner Park took Caanen with him to his ville.

"Let's have a drink," said Park as they walked through the dark village. Bits of thin newsprint swirled down the alleyway. Caanen ducked his head below the roofline. Chinese lanterns hung near the sliding door entrances. They entered a room lit with a weak incandescent bulb. He stooped slightly in order not to strike his head against the ceiling.

"Maekju and soju. Warm 'em up," Park said to the bartender.
"Aren't you going to go home and talk to your wife?" Caanen asked.
"No. I go home later."

The men sat down at a dirty wooden table. One could hear only the village generator with its slow boom-boom-boom reverberating in the dark. The incandescent bulbs in the room brightened and dimmed with each stroke of the generator. A young girl brought over drinks. An hour later two young women came and sat at their table. Park spoke to them.

"Mona will take care of you, Ru-tenent," said Park as he stumbled off with the other woman.

"You come home with me," said Mona, "you spend night with me."

Caanen followed the young woman down the alleyway past many shacks. The earth was firm and dry.

"We go here," she said pulling back a rice paper sliding door.

Caanen sat at the doorstep, removed his boots and stood within the small room. There was a bed, a small dresser and a sheet hung in the entranceway leading to the kitchen. He fell asleep on the bed.

"Wake up Ru-tenent," Mona said.

The alcohol had worn off and Caanen sat up. His first thought was what a ridiculous westernized name this Korean girl had chosen, "Mona"! She was at least five years older than Caanen.

"For God's sake," he said aloud, ashamed and chagrined.

"What is it Ru-tenent? We make love now?" she asked without expression.

∞

Later Caanen was aroused from sound sleep by Mona who was shaking his shoulder. He was naked. He pulled the comforter up to his neck uncertain as to what had happened earlier.

"You must go, now. Quick!" she said.

Caanen looked around. She had lit two small candles and the yellowish light reflected on the off-white rice paper covering the door. It was warm in the small room.

"You go now, or you be in trouble," Mona said.

Caanen looked at his watch, it was 5:00 AM. He needed to be back by Reveille or he would be reported missing. He quickly pulled on his uniform and boots and left, alternately jogging and quick marching the two miles back to Headquarters. He passed through the gate and the guard on duty came to attention and saluted as he jogged by. Caanen took a shower. Schuette was still asleep.

That evening Schuette sat on his bed and told Caanen that his wife was coming to Korea to visit him in three months.

"She'll be over here for two weeks. Maybe you could move in with Lehrer for a while?" he asked.

"Okay. Of course, I'll do that," Caanen said.

"We may go down to Seoul for a weekend."

There was a rapping on the front door. "Come in," said Caanen. It was Kim arriving for the Korean language lesson. The two men sat down at a desk and Corporal Kim opened his elementary school books. The lesson for the day involved a small child ice-skating with friends on a pond. Corporal Kim painstakingly corrected Caanen's pronunciation of Korean. Slowly Caanen was building up a sizable vocabulary. They finished the exercise by going over the alphabet.

As Caanen readied himself for bed that night he felt regret and shame for what had transpired the evening before, especially in light of Schuette's wife's imminent visit.

At the Officers Club the following evening Major Wilson let everyone know that he was returning stateside. He was being deployed to a Nike missile base in eastern Kansas not far from Caanen's home. Caanen insisted he look into renting his family farm since his parents had gone on sabbatical to France. Several weeks later Wilson's going away celebration took place. He quaffed a large amount of alcohol even though he normally did not drink. There was comradeship between him and the other junior officers—all of them had learned something about the Army and themselves under his kind, firm tutelage.

⁕

After removing the plates from the dinner table Park came up to Caanen who was still seated at his table. "You come my house tonight. Mona be there," said Park who stood before the soldier in his nightly uniform: a white longsleeved shirt, dark blue slacks with a belt several sizes too large and black, thin-soled oxfords.

Caanen realized as he walked to Park's village that he was brazenly flaunting the prohibition of officers fraternizing with Korean women. He felt a sudden chill up the back of his neck even though the air was warming in preparation for spring. As he walked alongside the frozen paddies, he was aware of a thundering cannon shot to the rear of him. The noise was repeated randomly as he walked along. These 'cannon shots' were from ice breaking apart on the Imjim River and continued for days. The ice was separating into large icebergs. The shots echoed up the granite-walled valleys from the river and reverberated off the mountainsides. It kept men awake at night in their huts.

Caanen walked to Park's favorite bar and waited. Park soon arrived and the two men smoked and drank for an hour.

"Come on we find your Yobo," slurred Park.

Caanen arrived at Mona's hooch. She was short even for a Korean woman and dressed in western garb. She offered Caanen a cigarette. He was uncertain what actually had occurred the last time they were together. Did he actually have sex or not? This was foremost on his mind as he wondered what had precisely occurred.

Mona was certain, however, of what she wanted. Later she confided to Caanen, "I don't like it here. Mamasan make me see too many men. Can you buy me house near camp?"

"What would it cost," he asked.

"Maybe $400, I be free," she said, holding tightly to his arm.

Caanen left the hooch early the next morning. As he walked back to HQ from the ville he noticed the sheen from the moonlight and the swathe of the Milky Way that lit up the rice paddies. He paused, lit a cigarette and languidly blew the smoke over his head, taking in the dark mountains at the sides of the valley and the endless patchwork of paddies receding into the distance. A Kim chi bus off in the distance moved along the roadway, its headlamps bobbing up and down as the vehicle slowly made its way towards him.

∞

Weeks later Caanen sat on the bed in Mona's quiet hooch. He could see out through the door where the sun was slowly retreating behind the small hills that formed the sides of the valley. Cool air closed in behind the shadows as they dutifully marched west. Mona replaced the lid on the soup after adding in a handful of small dried fish. She added some herbs and smiled at Caanen who lay on the bed reading.

Caanen felt happy. The poverty all around falsely assured him that he could have no selfish intent in his dealings with Mona. On the contrary he felt, his motives were romantic and generous. Nevertheless, he felt deep compunction about keeping a Korean prostitute. He knew at some level that this was immoral.

Caanen launched himself into the demimonde of Mona with goodwill and naiveté similar to the protagonist *Of Human Bondage*. However, it didn't end in tragedy as did the novel if only because Caanen was less personally courageous than the hero of the novel. He hid his liaison from Lt. Schuette. Caanen convinced himself of the romantic nature of the affair and perhaps believed not a little that he could reform Mona from a lifestyle she had been leading for more than 5 years. She was born into an impoverished rural family south of Seoul; her older sister had become a prostitute before her. She was infrequently visited by her younger four year-old sister whose presence caused Caanen much consternation. He felt his presence was compromising Mona's entire family. He repeatedly asked Mona not to have the child visit, little understanding Mona's need to remain attached to her family. Caanen felt Wan Sung Hi's Anglicized name, Mona, was improper and he could not bring himself to use it. Consequently, Mona became Sung Hi.

Korean women were an occasional dinner topic in the Officers' Club. Caanen knew of only one other officer with a "yobo." Captain Taylor had a yobo in the village and never joined in on the usual banter about women at dinner. Everyone with the exception of the Colonel knew of his local, off-base ménage. Back in Pennsylvania he had a pretty young wife and two children—Caanen had been shown their photograph one evening at the bar. Taylor's Korean yobo was conservative in her dress, never being seen in anything but a garment known as a hanbok that resembled a Japanese kimono with an obi. In the rural, impoverished areas of Korea women wore only classical dress. The prostitutes were the only ones wearing western garb thus advertising their availability.

Once a month a small, smartly dressed Korean man came to the Officer's Club with a valise full of Korean won. Officers queued to exchange dollars for won that they used to buy occasional maekju in the village and to pay their houseboys. A won was about half the size of a dollar bill and had more paper than the linen-impregnated American paper currency. Won, if carried in a wallet and folded over frequently, tore after several weeks. The moneyman had an amazing facility for counting out won, which exchanged at over 300 to a dollar. He held the wad of bills in one hand and with the other, rapidly riffled the bills stopping at precisely the right paper bill.

Colonel Carrick was present on these occasions to keep an eye on the proceedings—taking note of any officers who habitually exchanged large amounts of money. These officers might be dealing with Mamasans in the village or directly paying prostitutes. On one occasion Caanen wanted to collect some Korean dolls which were displayed in storefronts of nearly every village. These carved wooden figures were draped with traditional Korean dress and many of the dolls held musical instruments. The dolls were fastened on a wooden pedestal and encased in very thin, rectangular, fragile glass containers.

Caanen usually picked up Orientalia as he and Clark drove between Headquarters and the surrounding villages. Colonel Carrick closely monitored Caanen's monthly exchange of dollars for won.

Caanen relocated Mona closer to the battery and drew out the equivalent of $400.00 worth of won to pay for her move. The Colonel was unaware of the large withdrawal, but someone back in a small bank in rural Kansas realized that something was amiss. The president of Olathe Patrons Bank was on a first name basis with Caanen's parents and alerted his mother to the withdrawal with words such as "I hope he is putting it to good use" and "...one never knows what is going on overseas..."

Caanen later received a letter from his mother wondering if everything was okay—the bank had called her and said that he had spent a lot of money the previous month. Caanen reassured her that he was fine and there were no problems. Guilt began to mount within him.

֍

Mona was eager for Caanen to come early on a Sunday afternoon so that she could prepare a dinner for the two of them. She made a special trip by bus to Munsan to obtain an aromatic fish—small minnows dried in the summer sun. She also purchased a small amount of beef. Their hooch had two rooms. There was also a communal outhouse that Caanen never used. Four other houses were clumped together, separated by fences. Mona's small Pekinese patrolled the yard and the odor of dog feces met the visitor upon entering the yard through a flimsy gate. There were no locks on doors or gates, yet Caanen never lost any possessions that he brought to the house.

FROG CRACKS UP

The morning was bitterly cold once again and the creek that ran along HQ compound had thin shelves of ice along its banks. Caanen's boots cracked on the gravel spread in front of the Orderly Room. Williams was inside talking to Clark. Frog stood beside Williams.

"OK let's go," said Caanen.

"Come on Frog," said Williams. The dog trotted behind him with his flattened head and eye sockets pointing almost skyward. Clark drove Caanen and First Sgt. Williams to reconnoiter the Headquarters placement for an upcoming field exercise. Frog, sitting next to Williams, growled intermittently the entire way. Williams mentioned that he and Frog spent the previous evening at the NCO Club drinking.

An hour later they arrived at the site. Caanen got out and began to walk around the area. Williams remained in the jeep with Frog and Clark. By midmorning the sky was entirely overcast with gray, low slung dark cloud and the wind began to pick up from the north. Flurries of snow fell. Caanen gestured to Williams to follow him to site where the G3 van would be placed.

After walking for a short distance, Caanen turned around and looked for Williams. He could barely make him out in the heavy snowfall, now moving almost horizontally due to the stiff wind. Williams now began to gesticulate toward the jeep. Clark opened one of the canvas doors and Frog leaped out in a dead run for Williams.

Caanen could hear Williams encouraging Frog, "Come on Boy! Come on!" Frog never slowed his pace and left the ground about four feet from where Williams was standing. Williams began to flail with his arms and dance with his feet. Frog landed on his thigh with jaws open wide and remained attached to Williams as he thrashed the dog with his arms, trying to break the iron grip of his jaws. The animal held on until Clark and Caanen arrived and beat him off of the man with their fists.

Williams pushed the now cowering dog into the jeep. His thigh was bleeding in multiple spots. Blood spotted Frog's face. Williams compressed the wound with his fists to staunch the flow of blood.

"I guess maybe I'll have to do something," Williams said sadly looking at Frog.

"I guess you will, Top. He's going to kill someone unless you do," said Caanen.

NOW IS THE TIME TO SPEAK OF MAJOR PUFF

The new Battalion XO taking Major Wilson's place was unanimously and almost immediately disliked. Major Puff was short, bald, intelligent, and a fastidious dresser. He was 'earnest'. He meant what he said and he had an unwavering trust in the ways of the military. The major looked over the local rules and customs and disliked what he saw. He was disturbed by rumors that some of his officers were fraternizing with local women.

By then First Sgt. Williams was detailed to C Battery to serve once again with Lt. Reeves. He and Reeves celebrated their reunion. The two had been living in Charlie Battery for two months by the time Puff arrived. Reeves and Sgt. Williams along with the enlisted men settled into a routine that was anything but routine. The battery was the most isolated of the line batteries, nestled into the gentle slopes of a small mountain. The gun emplacements were at the talus of the mountain, each gun pointing due north. Like the other batteries it was surrounded by ten-foot high woven wire fencing with concertina wire draped over the top of the posts and at the base of the fence. Civilian guards policed the perimeter. Driving a jeep at a good clip took twenty-five minutes to travel from Headquarters to Charlie Battery. Reeves made a trek to Headquarters every evening to dine with the Colonel and other battalion officers, otherwise he was rarely seen by Caanen or the other officers.

Reeves and Williams were seated at the bar of Charlie Battery's Non-Com club one evening, the highest point in the compound. Given the isolation of the compound and the general laxity of discipline, Reeves and Williams met there each evening after Reeves returned from dinner at Headquarters.

"Well, Sir, I've hatched a little plan. What d'ya think? We could bring some ladies into the compound, a few of them, as long as they stayed in our club," said First Sgt. Williams, slurring his words.

Reeves leaned his elbows on the bar and lit a cigarette with his Zippo and twisted in one smooth motion on the stool to look directly at Williams.

"Sergeant...I say let's do it! Who'll know way out here. Just get them out by twenty-two hundred hours or we'll be court martialed," said Reeves with a burlesque wink.

"Right Sir. They'll be gone before midnight."

Within a month Reeves was often excusing himself from dinner at Headquarters. Upwards of twenty women were staying each evening on the compound, parceled out by MSgt Williams to the lower echelons of non-coms. Lt. Reeves had his own "yobo" who stayed for weeks in his hooch.

Major Puff began to suspect that something unusual was going on at Charlie Battery. In fact, he had a snitch--Corporal Dawson, his driver and only confidante. Dawson was slim, disheveled and bespectacled—he had no friends among the other officer's drivers. He rarely went to the non-com club but when he did, he paid careful attention to the conversations.

"Corporal Dawson any Battalion news?" Puff asked.

"Not much Sir. The men are complaining that Lt. Caanen can't seem to keep the theatre running. We haven't been able to see a movie in two weeks. Someone brought up an interesting tidbit last night in the club, though. I guess Charlie Battery has live-in maids now."

"What do you mean?"

"I mean Sir, that women are spending the night at Charlie Battery." "I see… Lay on a jeep for tonight at the motor pool," said Major Puff. "Where're we going Sir?" asked a smirking Dawson.

"Charlie Battery."

"Yes Sir, I'll let Motor Pool know we need the jeep." Major Puff showed his amateur status as a sleuth by letting another know his destination.

∞

Dawson pulled the jeep up to the Charlie Battery's main gate around 8:00 PM with Major Puff seated beside him. The infamous Private Butts was on duty in the guard shed (having been moved to Charlie Battery by First Sgt. Williams). He saluted and as the jeep passed through the gate to make its slow tortuous climb to the C Battery HQ he quickly picked up the field phone and informed Lt. Reeves that Major Puff had arrived.

Reeves walked out to greet the major's vehicle and saluted.

"Evening, Sir. Good to see you," said Reeves not in the least surprised. "Lt. Reeves…" Puff said looking around. He had been hoping to find the compound off guard. Before him at several hundred yards First Sgt. Williams was leading a platoon in calisthenics by the Non-Com Club.

"A little unusual for a Master Sergeant to be leading jumping jacks at night, isn't it?" asked Puff looking askance at the men struggling to move in unison and the older man moving erratically. Williams' legs and buttocks were badly atrophied due to drink and disuse and he presented a pencil-like profile.

"Sergeant Williams is unusual Sir. No doubt about it—he runs a tight ship." "I see," said Puff squinting at the men. "Can you show me around the compound?"

"Certainly, Sir. Happy to," said Reeves. The two men walked off toward the gun emplacements.

Thirty minutes later Puff slid into the front seat of the jeep. "Okay, Dawson. Let's go back to Headquarters. Something is fishy here."

MSgt Williams and Lt. Reeves stood at the entrance to C Battery to see Major Puff off.

"It's a good thing you rigged that up with the HQ Motor Pool clerk to let us know when anyone is headed out here," said Reeves to First Sgt Williams. "By the way, Top, don't lay it on too thick. I think Puff was a bit skeptical about you leading calisthenics."

This visit by Puff only whetted his appetite for more investigations. The fact that the top non-com was out leading calisthenics convinced him that everything was a façade. He concocted a foolproof scheme to capture Reeves and Williams *in flagrante delicto*.

"Alright Dawson I want you to get our sleeping bags, chow for overnight and a Battery Commander's scope and place them in the jeep along with some blankets. We are going out to Charlie Battery tomorrow night. Do not notify the Motor Pool about this."

"Yes Sir," said Dawson frowning. It was not his idea of how to spend a night.

※

The evening turned unusually cold and wet. Snow flurries streaked across the headlight beams as Dawson drove slowly to C Battery. The vehicle lights cast a shadowy world in front of them. Puff was contemplative and sat staring straight ahead. As the jeep made the climb up the final hill, Dawson turned off the headlights and turned the convoy lights on. The jeep was now moving down a decline facing the hill upon which C Battery was laid out.

"I can see the lights of the compound up ahead, Sir," said Dawson, "what do you want me to do?"

"Pull off here and shut off the lights. I'm going to set up the BC scope and see if I can see anything."

Major Puff extended the telescoping legs of the tripod alongside the jeep and mounted the scope on the platform. A cold wind came up the valley. Dawson and Puff shivered.

"Get your flashlight out and start taking down notes, Dawson?" Major Puff began to dictate out loud:

"Twenty-one hundred: no activity.

Twenty-one fifteen: no activity.

Twenty-one forty-five: a woman is entering the compound at the main gate in a kimono.

Twenty-one forty-six: the main gate guard is gesturing for the woman who just entered to leave the compound.

Twenty-one fifty: two women are leaving the non-com's club with Sergeant Williams and they're walking to the main gate."

Just then two young women dressed in white kimonos walked by the parked jeep having left the compound earlier. One of the girls called out to Puff, "Hey general, what you doing?"

Major Puff looked blankly at the young women with their heavy makeup and ghostly white garb shining in the night.

"It looks like their getting out all the women by twenty-two hundred hours, Sir, like regulations say."

"I don't believe it! Something is fishy here," said Major Puff. "Someone is letting them know when we leave Headquarters, Dawson. That's the only explanation for what's going on."

※

A week later Corporal Dawson and Major Puff repeated their nighttime sortie only this time Dawson told no one of their destination, neither the Motor Pool clerk nor the main gate guard. The two men drove to C Battery.

"All right Dawson pull over here and I'm going to set up the BC scope. You keep the log," said Major Puff.

"Right, Sir." Corporal Dawson brought the jeep to a halt on the declivity providing an excellent view of the compound sprawled out before them.

Major Puff set up the BC scope. The wind was brisk and the temperatures were in the thirties. Puff pulled up his hood on his parka and stamped his feet.

"Yea, just as I thought…start jotting this down Dawson.

Twenty-three thirty-two: four women entering the main gate and escorted by a non-com to the club.

Twenty-three thirty-five: My God! Another four women in kimonos are walking to the club.

Twenty-three forty: Now two women are walking from the main gate to the club."

Major Puff continued surveillance until early morning hours. By this time over a dozen women had been observed entering Charlie Battery and none had left. Dawson was cold and irritable each time Major Puff awakened him to act as scribe. Major Puff appeared indefatigable, clapping his gloved hands together and running in place to generate heat. The most noticeable feature of his face was the black-rimmed glasses that stared out from under the parka hood. Dawson was pitching from side to side in the driver's seat trying to get some sleep in the dead of night.

Major Puff carefully scanned the compound through the scope.

"No one has moved in the guard house for at least an hour—they're likely asleep. There's no movement in the compound except for the guards on the perimeter who are patrolling."

"Yes, Sir. I think we should head back now, Sir. Don't you?"

"Hell no! Start the engine. We're going to head directly for the officer's quarters and Sergeant Williams's hut. Hit it."

At the gate Major Puff stepped out of the jeep and peeked in the gatehouse. Private Butts was lying on the floor unconscious. They drove up to the entrance of the Commander's hooch. Major Puff rapped on the door and then forcefully opened it. He strode to the back of the hooch. Lt. Reeves was lying on his bed naked. A young girl cowered on the bed with her back against the wall and her knees up to her chin.

"Reeves! Lieutenant Reeves! Wake up. God damn it!"

Reeves rolled over in bed and groaned aloud, "What the hell is this?" Major Puff turned and walked out of the hut.

"Dawson run over to the non-com hooch and secure the door. I'll be there in a minute."

Moments later Puff walked to the non-com's hooch and pulled open the door.

"Sergeant Williams where are you," he shouted.

Williams poked his head out from the entrance to his quarters, "Sir?"

"I'm doing a bed check here. Have everyone step out here in the living area," said Major Puff.

The mess sergeant, motor pool sergeant, one gunnery sergeant and First Sergeant Williams walked out into the living space, each followed by a partially dressed Korean woman. The young women attempted to button their blouses and pull clothing about themselves.

"I want you and Lt. Reeves in my office at 0800 hours tomorrow morning. Is that understood?'

"Yes Sir!" said First Sgt. Williams.

DISGRACED

Dinner in the Officer's Club at Headquarters the next evening was attended by all the officers except Reeves. Everyone was acutely aware of his disgrace. There was little conversation at the three tables. Park was quiet and efficient in his service. It wasn't long before Major Puff began to speak in a hectoring tone. He spoke loud enough to be overheard at the other two tables.

"Discipline is very important when in combat. Precision of action is paramount and this only comes with training and discipline. We're going to restore that kind of discipline here," Major Puff continued. The room fell silent.

Colonel Carrick paused while eating and looked about at the others, trying to gauge their reactions and where he should place his sympathies. He was rattled by the righteousness of the Battalion XO and perhaps feared that one of his weaknesses would be caught out by the major. The junior officers returned to eating their meals.

The next day Reeves was reassigned to Headquarters Company. He stayed in the compound for several days and then left for Seoul. Caanen only had limited opportunity to talk to him. He was to be court-martialed and lose his commission.

"My wife and two kids can't live on a non-com's salary. I don't know what we'll do," said Reeves. Reeves had dreamed of commanding a field unit since the first day he joined the Army as a private. He was now leaving the service ignominiously. Caanen was saddened by Reeves's sudden departure. No one stayed to drink at the bar or play ping pong after dinner.

Colonel Carrick announced that Lt. Lehrer would be taking over command of Charlie Battery, replacing Reeves. His major task was restoring discipline among the men. Williams was to remain as First Sergeant. He was given a reprimand by the Colonel and absolved of any further responsibility for the activities that occurred in the hillside fortress.

A new officer was welcomed to the battalion that evening. Colonel Carrick and Major Puff went to great lengths to make him comfortable. The other officers wondered why. Lt. Roberts was pleasant enough, extremely quiet and appeared ill at ease with the other junior officers.

"Lt. Roberts will be our new G3. We need to get our training up to snuff and he'll be the one to do it," said Carrick to a group at the bar. Some of the officers who had been in Korea for half a year were jealous that a newcomer received this plumb appointment without any preparation. The G3 had a separate hooch with a houseboy, much like the battalion CO and XO. Within a day it became apparent why Carrick and Puff were so deferential to Lt. Roberts. He just graduated from West Point and after a brief preparatory stint at Fort Sill was assigned to the 1/17th. His father was a major general in Vietnam in charge of all land troops. Every career officer was looking out to make the proper connections—with several million people in uniform one needed all the luck one could find. The Army TOE (Table of Organization and Equipment) for field artillery units specified a Major or Captain for the G3 position, but it had not been filled for years—at least not since Vietnam was in full swing. Carrick was proud that he would be the only artillery commander in Korea with almost a full complement of officers under his command. He talked at dinner about increasing the training of the battalion with more complex firing missions. Lt. Samuels and the other Forward Observers regarded his comments with alarm. Samuels was the only black company grade officer in the battalion, a graduate of Ohio State University and the ROTC program. He had a robust sense of the ridiculous and was not afraid to make off-color remarks about the capabilities of GIs in Korea. He was closing in on the last of his assigned year with the 1st/17th.

"This G-3 better get going fast, I'm through sitting out in the woods with my black ass frozen off," said Samuels. Colonel Carrick glowered at Samuels. The other officers at the table smiled to themselves, knowing full well about Samuels's last Forward Observer outing where he never got out of his sleeping bag—calling in rounds while walking about with his sleeping bag wrapped around him.

Lt. Roberts came into the dining hall and everyone turned to greet him. He was short in stature and polite. Roberts's dress did nothing to enhance his appearance. In a setting where so much of a critical nature was decided in a quick glance, the West Point graduate fell woefully short—his fatigue trousers were not tailored, the shirt was blowsy and the trousers were held together an inch or so above the instep by an elastic band, not tucked neatly into the top of the boot. Colonel Carrick asked him to join him at the first table.

Captain Dobbins remarked to Wurtz that G-3 was such an important and pivotal position in Battalion operations that he couldn't see Roberts fulfilling this leadership position. "We need someone more dynamic than that!" he said.

Caanen talked to Roberts while in the club that first night and realized the young officer was not interested in gaining any mileage out of his father's name. Roberts had no more insight into what was going on in the military than did the other officers, he just wanted to fit in.

"What's the Colonel like," Roberts asked Caanen, "a real stickler for details or easy to get along with?"

"It's hard to say," said Caanen, "he's not a warm or open man."

As springtime progressed Caanen on a whim resolved to obtain a pair of young magpies and train them. A boy with the ubiquitous surname of 'Park' who hung around the main gate agreed to provide two young nestlings. The birds were regarded as good luck charms in Korea—not the troublesome vermin they were back in the States. Within several weeks young Park was at the front gate demanding to talk to Ru-tenant Canine. Caanen met him at the entrance and gave him three thousand won for the pair of young birds. He took them to his hut and arranged a nest within a wooden box. Scraps of food were provided from the officers' kitchen and the birds grew, soon fledging and flying within the hooch. Caanen named the pair Roscoe and Roy in honor of the recently departed Battalion XO, Major Roscoe Wilson and the current CO, Colonel Roy Carrick.

Schuette complained that the birds were messing on his bed and pointed to white droppings on his olivegreen Army blanket. Roscoe, in particular, was a headache. He was fond of flying to Caanen's collection of Dickens, standing on the spine of a book and pecking forcefully into the binding and loosening pages, ripping out a beak full of text along with the sought after glue from the binding.

Caanen walked to HQ in the morning with Roscoe on one shoulder and Roy on the other. They occupied themselves with pecking at various items on his desk, making off with pens, paper, clips, and trash out of the receptacles.

The villagers, meanwhile, were busy preparing the rice paddies for planting. They brought human ordure into the fields in large ceramic jars and emptied the contents into the paddies. The odor permeated the valley for several weeks. It was neither acrid nor sweet, but discernibly not the odor of animal dung.

Red, short-horned oxen pulled wooden plows in the softening earth coaxed on by men in bare feet with their white trousers rolled up to their thighs. Families were busy repairing the walls of the paddies. Life was quickening within the valley.

It rained heavily for over twenty-four hours. Caanen could hear the creaking of large icebergs in the Imjin. The small stream in front of HQ was swollen over its banks. He walked toward the Imjin River and saw the water flooding the lower valley from the recent rainfall. Large blocks of ice, the size of small houses were floating upstream towards the compound, scraping the rocks below as well as colliding into one another, tossing blue ice helter skelter.

At night Caanen met with Corporal Kim and the two worked late into the night.

Caanen was now able to write simple sentences in Korean script.

Some evenings Caanen went with Park to Kumkongni. The two drank maekju and ordered small side dishes of Kim chi. They always visited the same bar. Several bar girls were present in western dress and heavy makeup.

"Give me a cigarette, Caanen. Oh, here come yobo" Park said.

Caanen reached into the waist of his heavily starched fatigue shirt and handed Park the pack. Mona came up to the table in traditional dress and looked at Caanen.

"You no come to visit no more, why?" she said.

"Well, I can't just leave the compound." He was a little ashamed at his timidity in dealing with the prostitute, but shame and embarrassment were foremost when he dealt with Mona. By now he knew only too well that Mona was busy plying her trade with other GIs. Caanen felt he didn't measure up to the other officers who ordered the girls about, treating them like a commodity. He couldn't muster the will to treat Mona in the same way they treated their yobos.

SPECIAL WEAPONS

Colonel Carrick informed the battery commanders at dinner that he wanted an improvement in physical fitness among the troops. An officer in each battery was to take charge of leading calisthenics and running a mile each day. The junior officers at the nearby dinner table looked quizzically from one to the other. Most of the officers who obtained their commission through ROTC were out of shape or never had been physically fit. Officers who obtained their commission through OCS (like Caanen) thought they had seen the last of physical exercises.

Lt. Jacobs took a drag on his cigarette and blew the smoke toward the ceiling of the dining room. He had enhanced his small "tummy" since arriving at the battalion.

"God damn it, I don't want to do this," he said softly to the others at the table. The following morning Caanen was leading jumping jacks for the men at HQ. It was going to be a slow process, most of the men were too out of shape to complete the entire hour of exercise.

The Headquarters Battery XO was also Special Weapons Officer for the battalion. "Special weapons" was a term used for nuclear weapons. Caanen met with Major Puff to go over the responsibilities of the position. Puff set up a mock training exercise for the afternoon. Exercises were conducted regularly on a six-week basis. This consisted of an alert that was transmitted to HQ and involved all the line batteries as well. The Battalion XO opened a safe in HQ and the line battery officer opened a safe in his own battery Orderly Room. Each officer searched for the appropriate "cookie", a small square of numbered aluminum sheeting, crimped at its edges. The 'cookie" was then torn open. Inside the "cookie" were orders regarding further disposition, e.g., coordinates to fire upon or orders to abort the exercise. While this was occurring Caanen, along with two non-coms, was busy at a special weapons bunker assembling an atomic warhead to be fired from one of the 8-inch howitzers. Once there was congruence of the cookies at two separate sites, the Special Weapons Officer was then notified to stop assembly. However, there was always the possibility that the task would need to continue and that the three men would transport an armed nuclear weapon to a line battery.

The job of the Special Weapons officer was to read the manual of assembly out loud as two specialists put together either an ersatz nuclear round or the real thing—these were not labeled such but, were numbered and the assembly team was ignorant of which was which. The Special Weapons officer also was not privy to information regarding whether a real or dummy round was being assembled. The team met in an out of the way bunker in HQ Battery area. It was large enough to stand up in and had one incandescent bulb within a wire cage on the ceiling. The men worked rapidly. Caanen read the detailed instructions for almost an hour with such wording as, "Grasping the beryllium spacer with the left hand, turn the wrench one quarter turn to the right..." Invariably, after forty-five minutes of assembly a call was relayed from the XO's office to disassemble the round and return to station. Canaan was always visibly relieved to call the exercise to a halt. These exercises usually occurred during the night and the team was never able to fall asleep afterwards whereas, their comrades rested easily in their bunks, unaware of what was happening nearby or the gravity of the exercise.

*

Caanen took a jeep one weekend to tour the area around the battery compounds. He left in the early afternoon taking a snack prepared by Park. It was warm and the weather was turning sultry. Water still stood in the rice paddies even though the plants were now waist high. Caanen came upon a picturesque knoll stripped of all vegetation except for one robust Korean pine that sheltered a small Buddhist monastery. He drove up to the gates of the monastery. Decorative, clay lions lay on their haunches at each side of the main entrance comprised of a large wooden gate 10 -feet high and painted purple. The surrounding daub and wattle fence was coated with a brownish-yellow lime wash. Someone had recently raked the clay maidan and there were no footprints to be seen on the linear striations left by the rake tines. Caanen peered into the compound through slits in the gate. Nobody stirred. He went to the jeep, retrieved the snack and sat down at the edge of the maidan overlooking rice paddies that disappeared into the foothills, far down the valley that lay before him. Terraces made their way up the talus of each mountainside and bare earthen paddy walls formed a warp and woof that knit the viridian-green valley floor. A breeze rose occasionally, but the humidity soon caused Caanen to bestir himself and get back into the jeep.

Late that afternoon he drove in the opposite direction toward the Imjin River. He slowly made his way up a promontory that looked out toward Panmunjon. Night fell rapidly. Only Venus and a few stars were visible in the darkling sky. Caanen got out of the jeep and walked around to the hood and leaned back against it looking toward the sky. Suddenly there was shouting from below. Caanen walked toward the precipice in front of the jeep. Immediately, several rifle shots rang out from below. Caanen threw himself to the ground and made his way to the jeep. Several more rounds struck the cliffside in front of the jeep. He started the engine, turned on the convoy lights and slowly made his way down hill and sped toward battalion headquarters. Here was a reminder that in spite of the beauty of Korea, it was still a dangerous land.

DAILY LIFE NEAR THE DMZ

Colonel Carrick called Lt. Caanen into his office early one morning. Caanen had just awakened and was worried because the magpies had left his hooch the day before. The only sign of the birds was the destruction of *Pickwick Papers*.

"After the disgrace in Charlie Battery and Alpha Battery failing the last general inspection I am going to change some commanders. You're going to move down to Alpha Battery and I want you to get the place in shape fast. If I don't see appreciable progress within a month or two, I'll find someone to replace you as well."

"Yes, Sir!" said Caanen saluting. Caanen was proud that he had finally been given a command position, but it entailed risks as well. The battery might not improve its performance under his leadership. So many vehicles were red-lined that battery performance was unavoidably affected and unlikely to improve in the near future. He moved his gear from his HQ hooch down to the larger Quonset hut at the perimeter of Alpha Battery. He was alone in the building. An Executive Officer was due to be assigned to the battery in several weeks.

Alpha Battery was just across the roadway from HQ. It was a small triangular encampment. There were four large gun emplacements visible from the roadway. They were circular structures with earth mounded up ten feet in height and each mound accommodated one self-propelled howitzer. There was camouflage netting over the entire gun emplacement. Near the four gun emplacements was a ball diamond with a track around the perimeter of the field. Next to the main gate entryway was a small squat Quonset hut, the Alpha Battery HQ. First Sergeant Olivier was expecting the new CO's visit.

"Good afternoon, Sir. Welcome to Alpha Battery," said Sgt. Olivier, dropping his salute. Olivier was a man of medium height with curly, red hair and freckles. He possessed a critical intellect, particularly sizing up men. He and the heavy drinking First Sergeant Williams (now in C Battery) were the most senior and capable of the battalion non-coms.

Olivier had the battery fall in formation and introduced the men to their commanding officer. Sergeant Mainard came up to Caanen after the men fell out and introduced himself. Mainard was known throughout the battalion as its most knowledgeable gunnery sergeant, capable of getting top-notch performances out of his men. He was in his early thirties, handsome, a little stoop-shouldered with dark, closely cropped hair. Sgt. Park, in charge of the KATUSA contingent, introduced himself as well. He looked rugged and competent. The KATUSAs, who understood no English, appeared well disciplined.

First Sgt. Olivier was formidable, all things considered, particularly if he felt he had a rival to his authority. He stood 5'10" in paratrooper boots but, seemed much taller. His red-orange hair was cropped close to his skull. His forearms were muscular and freckled. His uniform was starched and prim, his boots had a mirror finish on the toe and his ball cap sat perfectly square upon his head. Olivier had been in Korea for a year by the time Caanen joined A Battery. The MSgt had also been without a commanding officer for 2 months and he was, therefore, *de facto* commander of the battery— every non-com and enlisted man was trying to curry favor with him. It was not easy to understand Olivier's moods. He was unpredictable in his favors. He got along socially with Sgt. Mainard. They met often in the Non-Com Club at Battalion HQ. and had an easy relationship. The other gun section sergeants were excluded from Olivier's immediate social circle. This was to have consequences in the future, particularly for Caanen. Twenty years of Army life had taught MSgt Olivier how to gain the upper hand in the enduring contest between the older, experienced non-commissioned officer and junior grade officers like Caanen.

"Well, Sir, shall I show you around the battery?" said Olivier. Caanen nodded and motioned to lead the way. Olivier headed toward the baseball diamond that had a running track around it. Beyond 1st base was Gun Emplacement 1 headed up by Sgt. Davis, a very large black man with voluminous clothing and ball cap a little askew who saluted Caanen sharply. He was the star of the opposing basketball team that Caanen played. More importantly, he knew almost a Sgt. Mainard about 8-inch guns.

"Welcome to Alpha Battery, Sir," he said. He bobbed his head slightly, smiling an acknowledgement that they had met before. He turned and went back to supervise his men.

They made the tour of the four gun emplacements, the last one was in the charge of Sgt. Mainard. He was crisp with his responses and it was clear that First Sgt. Olivier had a special liking for the man.

"Davis and Mainard are the best section leaders, Sir, but, Mainard has an affinity for these guns—this is the second 8-inch unit he's served in. When the guns go down, I go to him to get them back up again. This is the biggest problem out here, guns going off line. We don't have any ready replacement parts. Our Motor Pool is hopeless. It is under the supervision of Sgt. Bellwood who has been Article-15-ed twice on this tour alone for drinking.

Caanen now sat at the head table at dinner at the Officers' Club. There was little conversation with the taciturn Colonel Carrick. What little conversation there was, Major Puff provided. He explained the Domino Theory as it pertained to Vietnam and

Southeast Asia. It ran something like the following: Communism was a powerful force and the Soviet Union, in particular, was to be feared. Vietnam was an area of contention between Western culture and ultimately, the Soviet Union. It was imperative that South Vietnam remain in the orbit of Western influence, since if it fell to the Communists more and more Southeast Asian countries would align with the communists.

"So, the Domino Theory is a very real concept. It has little to do with us up here in the North, but this is why Vietnam is so important," Major Puff said. The younger officers thought of Puff as the "know it all" Major. The Domino Theory had merit, but advocates like Puff had the reverse effect amongst the younger officers who began to mock Puff's grand theory.

⁂

Lehrer and Caanen decided to walk to the Imjin River after dinner. North Korean agents were now active since the weather was less forbidding and the ice gone. Consequently, soldiers walked about outside of the compounds at their peril. The air was warm and there was little rain in the month of May. The two men walked along a deserted roadway encountering only a lone farmer returning to the village with his bullocks. They turned back toward the compound. Suddenly flames began to leap around the base of a large rick of rice straw stored under a thatched roof on a small farm alongside the road. The two men saw an elderly woman moving in a jerky fashion, her body profiled by the orange-yellow flames. She was bent over at the waist carrying pails in each hand. Local men soon joined her forming a line passing containers of water from one person to another. Caanen and Lehrer leaped over a wooden fence to join them in dousing the fire. The old woman's cattle were in a lot not far from the fire and lowing in fear. A fire bell rang in the village. Villagers snaked their way toward the farm through the rice paddies. The roof of the shed suddenly caught fire from the tongues of flame from below and the heat forced everyone to back away. The two officers were wet and covered with soot. The elderly woman walked about aimlessly. The shed and the straw were entirely consumed in the fire and collapsed into a solid ball of flame. Within ten minutes all that remained was a smoking pile of fibers with a glowing orange core. The smoke choked the bystanders. Caanen gave one last glance at the old woman who was silently staring at the orb of fire. He turned toward Lehrer and the two returned to HQ.

A US 2nd Infantry Division barracks was dynamited, June 1967

⚜

Schuette's wife came to visit for two weeks and Caanen moved to Alpha Battery to become Commanding Officer. Schuette and his wife had the hooch to themselves. He proudly ushered her into the Officers' Club the first evening and introduced her to 15 officers. His wife engaged in small talk with Caanen. She was alarmed at how barren Korea appeared with the mountains around the compound stripped of their vegetation and the crude roadways that went from village to village.

While Schuette's wife was in residence the Donut Dollies from I Corps came to visit HQ. Visits by these four American women occurred several times a year. The battalion officers were ordered to be present in the club in the early afternoon in dress greens to greet the guests. They talked with the women over coffee and pastries and stayed for the evening meal. Caanen felt ill at ease with the Donut Dollies and wanted to be loyal to his Korean yobo, who was, in his mind, more genuine and sincere then these young women visitors. He said little to them. Later in the evening he walked to Kumkongi to visit Mona. Caanen stood before her door for several minutes tapping on the doorjamb. There was no answer. He walked to the bar where he usually met her. One of the girls came up to him.

"Oh! She no here. She visit mother and sister in other ville. Okay?"

Caanen walked back to Alpha Battery ruminating on the veracity of the girl's response.

∞

Slicky Boys were a favorite topic along with "yobos" at evening mess. The most fanciful tales could not do justice to the capabilities of Slicky Boys; these thieves, stole Army materiel right out from under the eyes of US soldiers and always managed to escape. Caanen believed only half of what he heard and chalked the remainder up to exaggeration. He soon learned differently.

Colonel Carrick ordered a battalion training mission soon after Caanen was appointed Battery Commander of Alpha Battery. Because the battery lacked an XO, Caanen performed the duties of reconnaissance as well as making executive decisions. He and Specialist Davis, his driver, drove out to Kumgongni and then north toward the firing ranges leading the vehicles of Alpha Battery. As A Battery drove through the various villages greater numbers of slicky boys began to congregate at the roadside, recognizable by their white gym shoes, dark socks, black cotton trousers and white, long-sleeved shirts. These thin, lean men could not be confused with the "old guard" of Korean men in their traditional dress or with businessmen such as could occasionally be encountered in Seoul.

Caanen ordered the vehicle ranks to close up. A 10-ton ammo truck from Bravo Battery was lagging behind its company just in front of their jeep. Caanen picked up the PRC-10 handset and tried to raise Bravo Battery's commander to inform him of the wayward vehicle without any success. "This is Alpha 1. Out!" he shouted into the small device. He turned to hang the handset on the radio only to find a Slicky Boy twirling the final nut that held the PRC-10 to the jeep.

"God damn it Davis! Floor it now!"

Davis punched the accelerator and the thief could no longer hold on. Davis pulled the vehicle over to the side of the road away from any storefronts. Davis fastened the radio firmly to its metal frame mounting case once again. The two men got back in the jeep and looked up ahead and could not believe what they saw. Two Slicky Boys were jogging alongside the wayward 10-ton with wrenches in their hands and had successfully loosened the housing around the battery of the vehicle. It weighed 35 pounds and was positioned directly below the driver's side door. Davis gunned the accelerator again and honked frantically. The Slicky Boys continued to jog alongside the truck, appraising the situation calmly and then carefully stepped to the side of the road. They deftly disappeared down a crowded alley. The large battery bounded out from its frame and hung dangling by the cables until Davis could get the truck stopped.

"Sir, they're fucking all over the place. What are we going to do?"

"We're gonna close up ranks," Caanen shouted. "Pull the jeep over and let's wait until the convoy catches up."

North Korea fired fifty artillery shells from the DMZ at a ROK Army barracks, October 1967. (Major Daniel P. Bolger, *Scenes from an Unfinished War: Low-intensity Conflict-Korea, 1966-1969***)**

THE MOTOR POOL

F irst Sgt. Olivier lived in the non-coms Quonset hut with the Motor Pool sergeant, Sgt. Bellwood, an old looking 45-year old man. Bellwood had been in the service for over 20 years and was on his second tour in Korea. At least two times in the past he had been nearly cashiered for drinking. This was his third promotion to Sgt. 1st Class. He received the promotion upon re-upping in the Army back in the States and agreeing to a tour overseas. Caanen rarely saw Bellwood. He certainly was not in the chow hall in the mornings and only occasionally showed up at the non-coms table in the evening. Eighth Army was pressuring every command below it to become combat ready and was focused on the state of readiness of the vehicles. Due to the shortage of parts—the lion's share going to Vietnam—many of the heavier vehicles were inoperable a great portion of the time. In most cases this was due to a lack of critical spares and not misuse or poor maintenance. Caanen often wandered out to the Motor Pool to look over the vehicle maintenance records to ensure that periodic maintenance was being performed. Bellwood handed him the small three-ringed binder for the vehicle in question and Caanen would sit down and leaf through the pages. Bellwood invariably found reasons why he could not go over the books at the same time begging off by saying that one of the men needed him to help with a repair. Caanen knew the scuttlebutt about Bellwood, that he was incompetent and no one trusted his advice around the motor pool. On top of that, First Sgt. Olivier was so intimidating that Sgt. Bellwood was drinking heavily.

"I'll tell you Sir, Sgt. Bellwood is having a rough time of it. He's pretty hung over today," said Olivier in a calculated aside.

This made for a bad situation as Caanen could not just dismiss the sergeant for the simple reason he had no one to replace him with and an Eighth Army inspection was looming a month away. Caanen demanded the motor pool work overtime to "square the books."

The day of inspection arrived. Caanen met the inspecting team at the Battery Orderly Room. It was headed up by a full bird Colonel and Caanen was forced to entertain him for the better part of the morning. Sometime around mid-morning Caanen suggested that the two men make their way to the motor pool. As they approached the large metal building, the size of an airplane hanger, Caanen realized to his horror that disaster had struck. He stared fixedly at the large yellow metal building. In one of the vehicle bays a 10-ton ammo truck had been driven over the pits for the mechanics to inspect. It was not immediately evident at first glance that there was a problem, but the driver had driven the truck not only over the pits but, smashed through the back of the motor pool wall and the cab of the truck was protruding through the back wall of the Motor Pool. A superficial glance led one to believe the large truck disappeared into a recess in the wall of the building. Sgt. Bellwood smiled foolishly and nodded his head at Caanen who stood transfixed. Sgt. Bellwood walked around confidently, saluted the Colonel and began talking with the motor pool technicians—with an ease he never possessed before. Caanen suddenly realized that Bellwood was a little tipsy. Caanen shuddered as if his whole world was collapsing.

Caanen accompanied the Colonel around the different bays of the Motor Pool. He then realized that neither the Colonel nor any of the inspection team was aware of what had happened. Bellwood had opened the doors of the 10-ton truck and draped some sheets over them and fastened them to the wall of the building thus closing out any light that might enter through the gaping hole in the wall. The Motor Pool went about its business inspecting and providing records for the inspection team.

"Where's your fuel depot, Lieutenant?" said the senior officer.

"Over there, Sir." The two walked toward the enclosure within the compound of sandbags stacked to the height of a man. Above the sandbags was concertina wire. There was a wooden gate with several locks on it. Caanen opened them and the two surveyed the hundreds of 55-gallon drums of diesel and gasoline.

"You've got several that are leaking there. I'm going to note that in the report," said the Colonel. The two turned to walk back to the Orderly Room and await the other inspectors. Caanen glanced over his shoulder at the Motor Pool where he glimpsed the cab of the 10-ton truck protruding from the backside surrounded by metal strips that curled away from the building.

Later the Colonel wanted an exit interview with Caanen. "Well, Son," he said, "we're going to pass you with high scores—the only negative findings were the leaking 55-gallon drums of oil." Caanen looked around in disbelief, came to attention, saluted and said, "Thank you, Sir!"

That evening Lt. Caanen realized he had not written home for months. Although he was certain his father did not read any of his letters he knew his mother lived each day waiting for word from him. He wrote a short letter, ashamed that he been so selfish and concerned only with himself. He felt as if he had strayed from his "high principles" and wanted to start a new leaf. He wrote his parents a long "chatty" letter and closed with, "I love you and can't wait to be home."

A week later Caanen left Alpha Battery Orderly Room around noon and walked toward his barracks when there was a shout from one of the KATUSA guards at Main Gate, "Wook out, Sir!"

Caanen looked up to see a 10-ton truck bearing down on him. Dust billowed up from behind the vehicle. Caanen sidestepped to his left. The truck accelerated heading toward the baseball field. Caanen couldn't recognize the driver.

The truck slowed and began to circle carefully around the bases, slowly at first and then with greater speed. First base—2nd base—3rd base—home! The dust rolled outward from the ball diamond obscuring the horizon. Caanen shouted to the First Sergeant and both of them trotted toward the vehicle.

"What in the Hell is going on, Top?"

"I don't know Sir. That's Porter's truck. He's been trouble in the past, the fucking McNamara Special."

The two men paused several meters from the edge of the ball diamond. First Sgt. Olivier began waving at the driver. The truck slowed down and came to a halt between 2nd and 3rd base. The driver turned off the ignition and stepped out of the cab.

"God damn you, Porter! What the shit is this?" Olivier shouted.

Porter was agitated; his arms jerkily punctuated his speech.

"I felt like taking a ride, Sarge. I'm fine. I didn't hurt nobody. Can I smoke, Sir?" he asked while fumbling with the button on his shirt pocket.

"I'm not worried about you, you asshole. You've torn up the baseball field. You'll get an Article 15 for this if you're lucky. Otherwise you're going to the brig!"

Porter started to walk toward the mess hall. First Sgt. Olivier frowned at Caanen. "He's a McNamara special and high on something. I'll bet, PCP. Son-of-a-bitch!" shouted First Sgt. Olivier.

THE SWAP

Lehrer cautiously took over Charlie Battery. Reeves's short tenure as Battery Commander where allowing women to enter the compound had compromised many of the non-commissioned officers. Lehrer was suspicious of any Charley Battery NCO's ability to get the battery combat ready. First Sgt. Williams somehow escaped all culpability for the recent escapades in spite of the fact that Major Puff had observed him *in flagrante delicto* alongside Reeves with their 'yobos'.

Lehrer's most pressing problem however, was in discovering who was stealing Army blankets from the enlisted men and selling them to the local Koreans. There was always a brisk trade involving blankets, jackets, trousers and boots among the locals. The Supply Sergeant reported to First Sgt. Williams that he had issued almost the entire year's supply of blankets and he would have none left when winter began. Everyone was put on the alert to report suspicious behavior. Lehrer decided to inspect individual standup lockers reserved for each enlisted man. Each of the lockers was fastened by a combination lock. The inspection took the better part of an entire day. In the early afternoon, in the second to the last barracks, Lehrer approached PFC Henson.

"Open the locker, Private," Lehrer said.

Henson turned about and fidgeted with his combination lock, "I can't remember the combination, Sir."

"Take the bolt cutter to it, Sgt. Williams," Lehrer said.

The locker door burst open. Twenty blankets, neatly folded, fell slowly one after the other, onto the floor.

Lehrer called Caanen shortly after his discovery. "Everyone is mad enough to kill Henson. How about trading him off for someone in your battery. No questions asked.

How about it?"

"I've got just the person, Lehrer. We'll switch them out next week."

Private First Class Henson moved to Alpha Battery and Private (formerly, First Class) Porter was transferred to Charlie Battery. Caanen and Lehrer settled down to their friendly banter each evening at the officers' mess. Nothing further was said about the exchange until a month later.

One night Lehrer came to Officers' mess, visibly upset. He had just undergone an inspection by I Corps Motor Pool. The purpose of the inspection was to establish the combat readiness of the vehicles. One of the inspecting officers ordered the drivers of the two M-38 jeeps in the battery to undergo inspection. Lehrer's driver carefully drove the jeep up the slight incline leading to the vehicle "pits" which were in reality tracks suspended over a sharp declivity near the perimeter of the battery. All went well with the CO's jeep. Then Private Porter (of ball diamond fame) who had been assigned as the XO's driver, put his vehicle into first gear and rapidly drove out on the tracks and …. beyond. The front wheels dangled and spun over the end of the tracks. The jeep was delicately balanced on its midframe between tumbling head long into the gully and settling onto the tracks. Porter gingerly extracted himself from the vehicle.

Lehrer watched the entire catastrophe with the inspecting officer standing alongside him.

"Goddamn it, Caanen! That bastard may have cost me my officer's bars. What the Hell did you trade me?" Lehrer spluttered at the Officers' bar that evening. Pak served him a stiff whiskey and water. He swallowed the drink in one gulp.

⁂

Revenge for Lehrer came rapidly. Upon Henson's arrival in Alpha Battery problems soon arose.

The Battery Clerk reported to Caanen one Monday morning, "Sir, there is a problem in the Motor Pool."

"What are you talking about?"

"Sir, someone is shitting on your jeep. This is the second Monday in a row the Motor Pool has found human shit on the hood of your jeep."

Caanen walked towards the Motor Pool and looked for his vehicle. There was unmistakably a pile of human feces on the hood. The perpetrator had stood on the jeep hood, squatted and defecated.

"Jesus," Caanen said.

The morning excreta report became a regular Monday morning feature in HQ. The problem started suddenly without any obvious provocation and ended just as mysteriously—Caanen thought it likely due to Henson who returned stateside shortly after the last "shit" Monday incident.

⁂

One morning he was awakened early in the morning by First Sgt. Olivier who was shouting at the Officer's Quarters front door. Caanen arose and walked out in the hallway to meet Olivier.

"What is it, Sergeant."

"We've got to move fast, Sir. One of the men's been poisoned in Pamcogi. I've got the jeep outside."

Olivier drove the commander's jeep out of the compound and headed towards Pamcogi. It was a cool, placid morning, wisps of smoke drifted up from the villagers' chimneys. Olivier turned off the roadway and headed down one of the alleys in the village. He pulled the jeep up before a small crowd of villagers who formed a circle around a young Army private. The young man bounced awake, sat up and then staggered toward the jeep holding his head. The door of a nearby hooch was open to allow fresh air into the solitary room. An older Korean woman was helping a pretty young girl walk out into the sunlight.

"Goddamn it. No one seems to listen to our warnings about staying in the ville. Just last week there was a carbon monoxide poisoning in Bravo Battery. The same God damned thing. The soldier stayed overnight with his yobo and about did himself in," said Olivier.

The villagers returned to their homes and Olivier and Caanen took the young private back to Battery HQ complaining of a severe headache. Caanen thought back of the times he had spent at Mona's hooch. There would be hell to pay if he were caught groggy in the ville, having been overcome with carbon monoxide.

The sand embankments around gun emplacement #2 were deteriorating. New gunnysacks and additional sand were needed. The motor pool laid on for a 10-ton truck along with several 2 1/2 ton trucks that followed Caanen's jeep to the Imjin River early one clear morning. The convoy traveled several miles to a gentle curve in the riverbed where an enormous sand bar abutted the roadway. The vehicles turned into the moist sand dotted with weeds, shrubs and young willows. The men jumped from their truck beds and began filling gunnysacks with shovelfuls of sand and stacking them onto the 10-ton truck bed.

No one paid any attention to the fact that the tires of the 10-ton truck were slowly sinking into the sand bed. Fully inflated, the tires were the height of an average man. However, it was becoming increasingly easier to load the bags on the truck bed; the men did not have to lift the sacks as high.

"Sir, this truck is stuck for sure!" said Sgt. Davis. He stood to the side of the massive truck and shook his head. The driver attempted to rock the vehicle out of the sand to no avail. Caanen looked upstream at the massive river valley with its immense volume of water. "Would this enormous truck be swallowed by the river," he wondered.

The men grinned and walked off as Davis and Caanen stood by one another to determine what to do. Soon the men were wrestling and pushing one another into the cold Imjin River.

The driver was unable to extricate the vehicle from the sand even after unloading all of the sandbags. Caanen called for a Service Battery wrecker. Several hours later the 10-ton was winched out of the algal ridden water.

Sgt. Davis and the men transferred the bags of sand to the rescued vehicle and the entire work party left for the battery. They arrived just as dinner was being served. Caanen could not overlook the comicality of everyday life in the compound. He was never entirely convinced that the Army could fulfill its mission in Korea after experiencing events like that day.

Alpha Battery's officer corps was suddenly bolstered by the arrival of 2nd Lts. Wilson and Layland, the latter a young man from Chicago who was attending the University of Illinois when the draft caught him. Wilson was from Dallas and a recent graduate of the University of Texas. There were now three young men with time on their hands each evening after evening mess. Only Caanen brought reading material--he was reading *Pickwick Papers* for the second time.

Once a month the officers' mess was visited by salesmen from the Army PX. Amongst their favorite wares were various pistols and rifles. Some officers were fond of collecting firearms. Layland purchased a pistol and had the idea of constructing a firing range within the officers' quarters. He envisioned relaxing in the evening, sipping several beers and improving his shooting skills. There was, of course, neither TV nor radio, and the ville was strictly off limits for officers.

Layland spent several weeks assembling the ingredients of his firing range. He found a discarded couch and dragged it to the back of the Quonset hut. Sandbags were stacked in an arc 4 feet high near the back door. He commandeered an easy chair and placed it near the central space heater. He even found some out of date *Time* and *Life* magazines to thumb through. There was only one rule for use of the firing range: no one was allowed to fire a weapon who had drunk more than two beers.

Layland decided to inaugurate the shooting range and invited Lehrer to attend. Layland, Caanen, Lehrer and Wilson stood around the space heater in the back room. Layland opened cans of Vienna sausages and placed them on top of the space heater and the aluminum cans were soon bubbling and jumping on the iron lid. Houseboy Park served beers all around. Layland pinned some paper targets on the sandbags and stood back with his pistol to start off the firing.

"Five dollars to the winner!" Layland's first shot glanced off the concrete floor and buried itself in the sandbag.

"Jesus! This is going to be easy taking your money, Layland," Lehrer shouted putting down his beer.

An hour later Layland, Caanen and Wilson handed their IOU's to Lehrer and the group broke up.

The four men met once a week for months. Wilson, the new kid on the block, wanted to bring yobos to the firing range. With his boyish good looks, blonde hair and easy manner he was already the talk of the prostitutes in the ville. Caanen, who had witnessed the disgrace of Reeves said it wasn't a good idea and would bring Major Puff down on them. Wilson persisted and one evening brought several women to the hooch, one of whom crawled into bed with Caanen. Wilson hustled the women out of the hooch early the next morning. Caanen was angry and embarrassed. He ordered Layland to dismantle the firing range.

Lehrer and Caanen looked for ways to compete against one another as their batteries did in sports. Caanen wore a non-regulation piece on field exercises, a .38 special pistol. He had purchased it from Dobson when he left for stateside. It had a leather holster belt with a square silver buckle and he wore it around his fatigue jacket. He thought he looked very martial with the pistol, cravat and his long-billed ball cap.

Specialist Davis drove Caanen to Charlie Battery one morning. There were still patches of snow alongside the road and on the rice paddies. Caanen grabbed Clark's right arm suddenly and said emphatically, "Pull up and stop. I'm going to try and hit those crows over there!"

A small group of five crows walked across the frozen ground of a nearby rice paddy. Caanen opened the canvas side panel very slowly so as not to alert the birds. He poked out the short barrel of the .38 Special and slowly pulled the trigger. One of the crows, 50 feet distant, toppled over as the crack of the weapon echoed amongst the hills. Caanen whooped and ran toward the dead bird. He grasped the feet of the bird and laid it in the back of the jeep.

"I want you to take this over to Charlie Battery this afternoon and give it to Lt. Lehrer—tell him how I did it."

Several days later the Charlie Battery clerk delivered a small 24 x 24 inch sealed cardboard box with a label: "To Commander Caanen, Alpha Battery. Touché."

Caanen placed the box on his desk and carefully removed the tape. The edges of the cardboard buckled a little and an acrid effluvium escaped from the box. Inside were two dead crows.

LAPSE OF JUDGMENT

Caanen was jostled awake by First Sgt. Olivier. "I'll meet you in the office. We've got a mess on our hands," the sergeant said. Caanen, shaved, showered and dressed and arrived at the Battery CQ twenty minutes later.

"What's up Top?" Caanen asked.

"There was a fight in the Non-Com club last night. I just heard about it from Sgt. Mainard. Everyone was drunk and several guys got into it and Mainard tried to break them up. He hit a private from Bravo Battery with a baseball bat on the head. Not directly. The private didn't lose consciousness but, was taken to the hospital at Camp Casey."

"Is he okay?" said Caanen.

"Yea, he's fine. It's what to do about Mainard. This could come to a General Court Martial. He's so important to our mission we can't allow that to happen. Besides, he has a wife and 3 children at home in Tennessee and can't afford a cut in pay grade," said Olivier. "I think we need to prepare an Article 15 against him and it may prevent the General Court Martial."

The next several hours were spent preparing the paperwork for an Article 15. Sgt. Mainard presented himself before Lt. Caanen and Caanen read off the charges of causing a disturbance on base. Mainard listened and then concurred by accepting the Article 15— it included a fine that he would pay over 6 months. There had been no discussion with Sgt. Olivier that what Mainard did was perhaps a felony. Everything was being done to "save" this man from being punished by the legal system. The victim was released back to active duty after a two-day hospital stay.

Later in the day the Battalion Commander called Caanen and asked why he had intervened with the process and given Mainard an Article 15; the Colonel said he was going to void the Article 15 since what had occurred rose to the level of a General Court Martial offense. Injuring another soldier was not a simple act to be dealt with by fining the culprit. The Commander understood Caanen's attempt at standing by Mainard and he even sympathized to some extent but, he was insistent that this be sent to General Court Martial.

A month later Mainard's trial was held at Camp Casey. LTs Caanen, Lehrer and Layland all testified on behalf of Mainard. After several hours of deliberation, the verdict was read by one of the Adjutants. Mainard was busted to private first class, a drop of three pay scales and reassigned to a fort in Kentucky. For the entire month Caanen endured the snide comments of Lt. Lurch of Bravo Battery who said it was a travesty of justice that Mainard did not go to prison; what he had done Lurch said was out and out criminal. Caanen realized to his shame that he had been overly influenced by MSgt Olivier's explanation of the event and had not entertained any alternative stories other than Olivier's.

THE MESS IS INSPECTED

Caanen was keen on making improvements in some of the battery buildings to boost morale. He decided to spice up the chow hall by putting wainscoting in all of the main rooms along with terrazzo floors. Terrazzo was surprisingly cheap in Korea and there were many craftsmen in villages. Caanen met with a "contractor" from Pamcoghi and the two men haggled over "costs." The wainscoting was pine with "burnt" highlights and the terrazzo was a red, cream, and green mix with brass dividers between the two-foot square sections.

First Sgt. Olivier was skeptical about the entire project. "Sir, if the Colonel finds out about this, you're going to be in the shit, no doubt about it. Giving the Gooks the metal treads from the guns, whether or not they are of any use is going to lead to problems"

Caanen agreed to exchange one truckload of used treads that had been stripped from the guns to underwrite the entire project.

⁓∞⁓

Mess Sergeant Woods was on his third tour in Korea. He was a soft spoken, gentle man with a sizable paunch, balding forehead and anxious about every meal he served. A routine meal with a simple menu of meat and potatoes caused him consternation. He married during his first tour in Korea and his wife lived with their two sons in Pamcogi. Woods was given permission to live with them. He had little interaction with the other servicemen since he lived off compound with his Korean wife and children.

Caanen received word late one afternoon that there would be a snap inspection of Alpha Battery by an officer from Seoul. First Sgt. Olivier called a Battery formation and informed the men of the imminent inspection. Woods came up to Caanen with a worried look on his face.

"Tomorrow our menu calls for turkey and dressing. I don't think our cooks will handle this too well," Woods said.

"Well, you've got almost 24 hours to prepare the meal, surely you can get things together by then," said Caanen.

The following day, one hour before chow call, a waxed and polished jeep arrived at the main gate. The license plate was crimson with two large embossed gold stars. There were two aerials projecting from the rear bumper, 15 feet long and undulating slowly from side to side.

1st Lt. Caanen and First Sgt. Olivier double-timed to the gate, came to a halt and stood at attention and saluted.

A short, stout man stepped out from the passenger side. He had a polished helmet liner with two stars. The most conspicuous part of him was the holster belt he wore over his fatigue jacket with ivory-handled pistols on each hip. Caanen wondered if he were dealing with an incarnation of George Patton.

"Good morning, Sir. Let me show you around the compound," Caanen said. "Do you know why I'm here, son?" asked General Waxman as he lit a cigar. "No Sir. I don't."

"I suspected you didn't. Well, you're the closest unit to North Korea that possesses nuclear weapons in this God Forsaken country and I want to make sure security is adequate and that you're battle ready," said General Waxman.

The two toured the compound. "It looks like you've done a good job getting things squared away here. Let's go to the mess hall. I'd like to inspect the kitchen. The Army runs on its stomach."

Sgt. Woods met them at the main doorway to the mess hall. His white apron was stained with gravy drippings. One of his trouser legs had fallen outside his boot. He saluted the general bringing his fingers up to his cook's cap and moving it a little askew.

General Waxman glared at the man. "What's for dinner sergeant," he said. "Turkey, Sir. Mashed potatoes, and dressing, Sir," Woods sputtered out. He was terrified by the small man with the shiny sphere on his head.

"Let's go see your ovens," the general said striding toward the kitchen. The enlisted men in the chow line turned to stare at the visitor.

The General, Caanen and Woods paused as they were about to enter the kitchen through the swinging doors.

"All right, Sergeant what temperature do you cook your turkey?" the general asked leaning toward the non-com with his hands on both pistol handles.

"'til it's done Sir!" said Woods, visibly trembling.

General Waxman squinted at the man. He knew he could catch him out on specifics. "How long have you been a cook, Sergeant? The manual tells you that you heat the bird until the core temperature is 170 degrees. Go get the manual!"

Sergeant Woods looked blankly at the general. Finally, he turned and went through the swinging doors. The General engaged in small talk with Caanen and waited. The enlisted men in the chow hall were now staring fixedly at the two men. Ten minutes later Sergeant Woods had not returned.

"Go get that man!" the General shouted.

Caanen went into the kitchen office and found Woods pulling manuals off the shelves and sorting through them.

"I can't find it, Sir. I can't find it," he said weakly.

"C'mon Wood just go and talk to him. Show him what you know and he'll stop this crap," said Caanen.

"I'm so nervous I can't talk," said Sgt. Woods.

The general approached the two men.

"Let's have a taste of one of your birds," said General Waxman.

The general entered the large kitchen and the men at the stoves came to attention. "At ease, soldiers," said the general. He took a carving knife and sliced off some breast meat after ordering the soldier to remove the turkey from the oven.

"That one's not done yet, Sir," said Woods.

"You're one poor fucking cook, I'll tell you, Sergeant. This turkey isn't done!" Caanen said, "Well Sir, Sergeant Woods was trying to tell you that."

The General turned his head and skewered the young officer with one eye. Later as he climbed into his jeep after finishing the inspection, he gave Caanen a menacing look, his dark eyes peering out from under the helmet liner.

"That mess sergeant of yours is a joke! You better see that he is relieved of his duties."

THE *PUEBLO* AND THE BLUE HOUSE

January 1968 was cold and miserable near the DMZ. It was a momentous month in the history of the young Republic of Korea.

January 11, 1968

The *USS Pueblo* left Sasebo, Japan with orders to conduct surveillance of Soviet naval activity in the Tsushima Straits and electronic transmissions from North Korea. On January 23, 1968, The Pueblo was boarded by the Democratic People's Republic of Korea and escorted to Wonson. [The ship is moored in Pyongyang on the Taedong River to this day and is a major tourist attraction.]

However, the incident led to Kim Il Sung re-evaluating his policy after discovering the bond between the US and ROK became stronger, not weaker. (Major Daniel P. Bolger, *Scenes from an Unfinished War: Low-intensity Conflict-Korea, 1966-1969*)

The Pueblo Incident led to weekly exercises for Special Weapons officers in I Corps. Fortunately, the small square aluminum "cookies" when torn open terminated the exercise and the *status quo* returned. The tests were run in the early morning hours, terrifying the officers as they rushed to get on their clothes and gain access to their Special Weapons bunker in the bone breaking cold of the underground bunker.

January 19, 1968

Thirty-one North Korean rangers infiltrated the DMZ and headed for Seoul. Lt. General Kim Cong-tae told them, "Your mission is to go to Seoul and cut off the head of Park Chung Hee." (Major Daniel P. Bolger, *Scenes from an Unfinished War: Low-intensity Conflict-Korea, 1966-1969*)

ROK and US units were placed on 24-hour alert after North Korean infiltrators were discovered outside Seoul. They arrived in Seoul in small groups riding Kim chi buses. These guerillas were given a password to re-enter North Korea but, none of them would ever use it. Kim Il Sung dreamed up this mission confident that the US puppet government in Seoul would fold under attack. Instead, the infiltrators were discovered before they made it to the Blue House and a countrywide manhunt began. Guerillas were killed on almost a daily basis and pockets of guerillas were found and destroyed north of Seoul.

Caanen and the other line officers of 1/17th checked the battery perimeters each night. Naked incandescent bulbs shone from 18-foot poles onto the thin layer of snow. The wind bit into one's face. Caanen wondered how the infiltrators remained alive as they walked crazed with cold from one foothill to another with little food or hope of making the DMZ. On January 28, Caanen was awakened by Sgt. Olivier who said that ROK units were in the area and had cornered two infiltrators south of C Battery compound. The ROK Commander wanted to meet with Caanen.

Lt. Colonel Kim was dressed in woolen fatigues. His helmet was strapped tightly to his chin. He was taller than most Koreans, appeared very fit and spoke impeccable English. He informed Caanen, with Sgt. Olivier beside him, that he had run to ground two infiltrators about two miles south of the battery. The men were on top of a small hillock, barren of trees. Col. Kim had a rocket launcher on his jeep and proposed using it.

"Let's give them the opportunity to surrender Colonel," said Caanen. "I'll go out there with you."

Caanen left with Col. Kim. The sun was out and its rays glanced off the snow and ice alongside the road. They arrived at the site where the guerillas were holed up: a small hillock of rock directly in front of them, perhaps 400 yards. The jeep was soon surrounded by a phalanx of ROK soldiers.

"They're up there at the top, dug in," said Colonel Kim who was holding a bullhorn.

Kim raised the bullhorn and spoke slowly in Korean, offering the intruders the opportunity to surrender. The response of the two men was to roll a grenade down the hillside that came to a stop against a boulder and ended in a small, ineffectual explosion. Kim gestured to his driver who then removed the cover from the rocket launcher. He sighted on the hilltop. Caanen and Kim were soon engulfed with smoke from the rocket launch and almost instantaneously there was a loud explosion. Rocks and clothing sailed through the air at the top of the hill.

Kim used the bullhorn one more time. There was no response. The platoon of ROK soldiers started up the hillside to verify the death of the last of the infiltrators.

Caanen returned to his Quonset hut emotionally drained. The terrorists were dead now but, the rapidity of the destruction was apocalyptic. There was no going back and discussing alternatives. It was faintly reminiscent of the death of the brass pickers shortly after Caanen's arrival in Korea. Life seemed so cheap here in the Chosun. Things returned to normal after January.

SEOUL

Lehrerer and Caanen were granted a three-day pass to Seoul. They left their respective compounds in mufti early one morning and took a Kim chi bus to Seoul. It took six hours, what with frequent stops and changes of passengers. The two disembarked in the Old City center after entering through the East Gate. Light rain fell. It was dusk and moisture was visibly rising from the street surfaces. Incandescent bulbs hung outside in the rain over the entrances of the restaurants and hotels. Everywhere the two walked there was the smell of coal smoke, grilled meat, Kim chi and urine. Lehrer proposed eating and then finding a hotel. They entered a busy looking restaurant. The odor of alcohol, soy and spiced grilled beef permeated the air along with cigarette smoke. The two officers removed their shoes and stepped into a separate dining room closed off with rice paper sliding doors where they were attended to by a young waitress who knew little English.

Caanen ordered for both of them, "Bulgo-gi with noodles and soup." "I don't want any dog meat!" said Lehrer.

The waitress brought in a cast iron brazier laden with red-hot coals. She set aside a brass tray with sliced sirloin, scallions and peppers. She also brought in smaller trays of white rice and Kim chi. The two men began to drink warmed soju and the waitress sat down beside them and grilled the meat, deftly flipping it with chopsticks.

Caanen had become very proficient in the use of chopsticks with Mona's help over the previous year. Lehrer was struggling with them.

"I get you fork, Ru-tenant," said the waitress.

After the meal the two men walked several blocks and obtained rooms in a hotel. The foyer was lit with a weak naked bulb. It was difficult to read the ledger on the counter. There was no bellhop. They walked to the fourth floor and entered their rooms with their travel bags. Shortly after Lehrer knocked on Caanen's door.

"I say we get a massage and a bath tonight. The concierge knows where to go." Twenty minutes later they entered an enormous, high ceilinged room, easily the size of a small gymnasium. The two men were blinded by the dense steam coming off the bathing pools. A petite, attractive young woman in Western dress approached the men and took Caanen by the hand.

"You come with me," she said.

Caanen followed the girl. He looked around and could make out neon lights on some buildings through the large glass windows that encircled the room. Otherwise all one could see was the steam rising to the high ceiling. Each individual bath area had a massage table with retractable curtains surrounding the table. Each bath was sunken 6 feet below the floor surface and lined with smooth granite stones. The water in the bath was a foamy emerald color barely visible through the steam.

"You takee clothes off and lie down table," said the masseuse entering through the steam. She turned her back to Caanen. She had on a white barber's jacket and dark slacks with low cut tennis shoes. She turned back toward Caanen who was now lying on the massage table with a towel wrapped around the waist.

"You relaxee, GI. No kenchanaaah… (meaning, "no sweat") she said, confident that there would be no objection. Her practiced hands began kneading his thighs. Caanen was soon swooning with the heat, moisture and the soju. He could barely rise from the table minutes later, drugged by the sensuality of the massage and having just ejaculated through the professional services of the young lady in tennis shoes. He stepped into the steaming bath and submerged himself hoping to regain control of his near delirium. Later, he shamefacedly stepped out of the bath and wrapped himself with a towel.

"Lehrer, where are you?" he called over the canvas divider.

"Jesus, Man! Over here! Don't disturb me. I'll be with you in a minute," said Lehrer.

༺༻

They spent hours the following day at the National Museum looking at pottery and then dining out later. Lehrer frantically flagged down a taxi late in the evening to take them to Walker Hill. It was a western style resort high on a bluff alongside the Han River. The driver careered down the entrance drive and skidded to a stop just before the 10 o'clock curfew. The men gave the driver a handsome tip. A doorman assisted them with their meager luggage.

Caanen and Lehrer awakened late next morning and had a leisurely breakfast. They walked the perimeter of the resort overlooking a broad sweeping curve of the Han river. Caanen looked toward the far bank where a few scattered buildings dotted the river valley. A large levee was being constructed. Hundreds of men and women pushing wheelbarrows loaded with soil could be seen toiling along the levee and eventually discharging the contents of the wheelbarrow on the river side of the levee. There was one wheezing steam shovel operating alongside the army of wheelbarrow drivers. Further north, concrete pylons were being poured in the river in preparation for bridge construction.

The concierge approached them, "Would you like to meet girls?" he asked politely. "Girls have rooms at resort. I show you?"

"Let me have a whiskey and water first, then show me the way," Lehrer said without hesitation.

Hours later Caanen followed the concierge to a room far removed from the center of the hotel.

"Wait here," said the concierge and carefully pulled the door shut. There was only a bed and nightstand with a lamp in the room. Caanen sat on the bed. There was no pillow.

Two young women were led into the room by the concierge. Both politely bowed toward Caanen.

"I bring maekju," said the concierge bowing and walking backward with a large smile on his face.

One of the girls said, "we go bed now?"

"Wait, my friend is returning," said Caanen, embarrassed as one of the girls sat down next to him, putting her arm around his shoulders. Where in the hell is Lehrer? Caanen thought.

Lehrer entered the room, sized up the situation and put his hand out for the other girl. He took several packets of condoms out of his pocket and tossed them toward Caanen, "here take these."

Twenty minutes later Caanen's girl pulled on a slip and left the room. Caanen squeamishly removed the condom from his shriveled penis and stared at it wondering if he should lay it in the glass ashtray. There was no trashcan in the room. Finally, he rolled over and placed it under the bed. He wondered later if there were other condoms there or was he the only prudish and fastidious man who had used that room.

Later that afternoon Lehrer and Caanen boarded a Kim chi bus for home. Lehrer continued sipping whiskey. Caanen felt nauseous and tried to close his eyes and lean against the window of the bus. It began to rain and the rivulets of water sliding down the glass made Caanen feel unbearably sad.

EACH DAY BECAME
AN ETERNITY

Weekends seemed interminable as time dragged on. The enlisted men were in the club by noon and most of them inebriated by two o'clock. Caanen read or occasionally went to the Officers' Club and played ping-pong. His Dickens' collection was tattered and worn. One particularly slow Saturday Lehrer arrived at the Alpha Battery Officer's Quarters.

"You wanna go to the club?" Lehrer asked Caanen.

"No. Let's stay here. Are you hungry?"

"Sure."

Caanen took a small tin of Vienna sausages, popped off the top and placed it on the top surface of the space heater—the officers' favorite snack.

"Puff is getting on my nerves talking about the Domino Theory every night at dinner. I'm sorry, I don't believe that it is a viable explanation at all, do you?"

Caanen lit a cigarette and stirred the bubbling sausages with a fork. "No and everyone else is tired of his hectoring. I've an idea how to get even with him. Let's call his quarters through a field phone."

"If we get caught it's going to be our nuts. He's going to try and find out who did it."

Caanen got a line through to Major Puff.

"The battalion operator won't know where the phone is coming from. We'll just use heavy accents," said Caanen adopting a Southern accent.

"Hello, this is Colonel Hill from I-Corps calling for Major Puff. Hello Major Puff, I'm G-2 here at Santa Barbara and wanted to talk to you about strategy. The commander said that we should get in touch with you about Vietnam.

"Well yes, I served one tour there. How can I help you?" Puff responded. Caanen continued with a phony Southern accent, "We hear that you are really pushing the fuckin' Domino Theory regarding Asia. I've lived in Asia and I wanna tell you, you've got your head up your ass!"

"Who is this calling?" shouted Puff. Caanen started to laugh into the phone and immediately hung up the receiver.

Once Caanen and Lehrer had stopped laughing they became apprehensive about their prank. What if Major Puff were to discover the whereabouts of the field phone. Dusk was settling on the compound and it would soon be time for supper at the Officer's Club.

"Come on, march order that phone Caanen and let's get out of here. The best thing is for you and I to beat it up to Battalion and hang around until Puff shows up at the Club. Come on!" Lehrer said grabbing his fatigue jacket and pack of cigarettes. Major Puff was present at dinner but, made no mention of the phone call.

❧

Each day was an eternity. Two months passed uneventfully. Army life took its inevitable course.

GOODBYE TO CHOSUN

Caanen and Lehrer were scheduled to go stateside together. A gathering at the Officers' Club the evening before their departure commemorated their exits from Korea. Pak was behind the bar, voluble and rapidly pouring drinks—events like these were a cause for rejoicing. Caanen was a favorite amongst the officers' club staff—his feeble command of Korean a reason for some pride since it demonstrated that the occupying Army were not all chauvinists—Caanen was thought to be 'simpatico'. Lehrer, more aloof, had performed the impossible, re-installing discipline and respect in Charlie Battery. When he took command, it appeared hopeless that anyone could revive the battery from the chaos it had sunk into after Reeve's short tenure as commander.

The usual perfunctory goodbyes were made at the ceremony and then Layland presented Caanen with a 'present.' Caanen removed the wrapping slowly, fearing that an embarrassing moment was at hand. Yes, there it was, a photograph of Mona sitting on her bed holding her Pekinese puppy. She appeared small, awkward, unattractive. Caanen flushed, said thank you and placed the photo on the bar behind him. His mind reeled in spite of the smile on his face. Caanen drank Pak's concoction and prayed he could regain his equilibrium.

In his hooch later he thought, 'Was I in love with that person?' The very name, Mona, provoked flashes of guilt and shame. 'I think I was seduced by the poverty of this country and my constant romanticizing of the situation. That was the genesis of my fall from grace.'

COMING HOME

It was raining at Sea-Tac when Caanen arrived. Two years before when he left the airport for Korea it was raining and here it was raining again. A bus transported the soldiers to Ft. Lewis and Caanen stared out the window looking at the small redwoods and other evergreens that formed a perimeter around the fort. He spent two days standing in line with other officers and processed out of the military to be restored to civilian life. It was somber in the officers' quarters; no one wanted to strike up a conversation; everyone was thinking of his travel home. 'I'll be back in Kansas City in a matter of hours,' Caanen repeated to himself.

When Caanen landed in Kansas City his parents met him at the plane. His mother tried not to cry and grimaced with a smile as she wrapped her arms around him. His father shook hands as he greeted him.

"I'm glad you are home son," his father said.

"Yes, I am too Dad. I'm not entirely sure what happened to me in the last three years."

Caanen gripped his mother in his arms and squeezed tightly. It was a windy August day.

EPILOGUE

Forty years later Caanen and his wife left Cologne, driving along the Rhine. They stopped for several days at Koblenz. It was late in the summer and the weather was splendid: sunny and warm during the day and the evenings were cool. They sat outside at restaurants and sipped digestifs. One day was devoted to crossing over the Rhine, sketching the gorgeous rose-stuccoed Baroque castle by Balthzar Neuman at the foot of Ehrenbreitstein and then climbing the steep roadway to the fortress. This was the very same fortress on the coat of arms of the 1/17 Artillery Battalion. Ehrenbreitstein is massive, the second largest fort in Europe and much of it underground. As one walks the grounds the fort's impregnability is very convincing. As the two tourists walked along the fortress wall facing the Rhine they discovered a bronze *bas*-relief of a young soldier from the Deutschland Division, his head covered by the distinctive World War II German helmet. The young soldier was presented in profile; his eyes closed. This death mask was a simple memorial to the mothers of Germany who suffered in silence after losing their sons in World War II. Caanen thought of the pain and fear his mother endured years ago when he foolishly allowed himself to be drafted into the Army, leaving things to chance rather than exerting himself in school.

From the height above the great rivers Caanen looked out over the parapet at the silently flowing Mosel and the Rhine rivers. The sun shone on the green riverbanks and sightseers could be seen walking around Deutsches Eck, a massive monument to Wilhelm I who, adorned with a helmet and mounted on a bronze steed oversaw the confluence of the rivers. Deutsches Eck was very much a monument to the military way of life, once of importance to Nietzsche and Caanen as well. The commitment to the masculine art of soldiering with its rigid code of conduct had only one purpose, defeating whatever enemy lay ahead. Caanen was imbued with this culture upon entering the Army and he still felt a pang thinking back at his spotless integrity when he entered the Army. Sure, he achieved a certain success as a leader of men—he definitely had a knack for it— but, later the young officer began to see the reality within which he lived, not the romantic dreams. There were the needless deaths of brass pickers on an artillery range, a young man bludgeoned by an angry sergeant, and a Slicky Boy ground under 8-inch gun treads. His thoughts then went to other things that happened in Korea. What about keeping a paramour in the ville? There was no moral justification for that even though he had stumbled into the relationship. It never seemed right at the time and certainly it did not seem right many years later. Yes, Caanen had made mistakes and poor choices and it softened his approach to acquaintances and subordinates in the years ahead. Maybe he should be thankful that he could now tolerate the missteps of others without condemning them. He certainly was no longer the haughty, leader of men he once thought to be the pinnacle of manhood.

It is curious to relate that many years after leaving Korea Caanen could involuntarily be transported back in memory to a little chop house in Pamcogi, not unlike Proust eating a madeleine in *Remembrance of Times Past*. Decades later, the taste of the spicy cabbage, kim chi, could bring memories flooding back to Caanen. He envisioned himself sitting at a diminutive dilapidated table, chopsticks in hand with a steaming rice bowl before him. Kim chi was his madeleine.